INVESTING IN FINANCIAL MARKETS IS **NOT** A ROCKET SCIENCE

INVESTING IN FINANCIAL MARKETS IS **NOT** A ROCKET SCIENCE

Investing Knowledge Simplified

BALAJI RAO D G

PARTRIDGE
A Penguin Random House Company

ISBN:	Hardcover	978-1-4828-4783-3
	Softcover	978-1-4828-4782-6
	eBook	978-1-4828-4781-9

Print information available on the last page.

To order additional copies of this book, contact
Partridge India
000 800 10062 62
orders.india@partridgepublishing.com

www.partridgepublishing.com/india

Acknowledgements

I am thankful to all these people and organizations who have been directly and indirectly instrumental and also responsible for me to gain ample knowledge of financial markets without whom all my endeavours would have been meaningless.

To,

My parents, my younger brother Harish Kashyap, my wife Mamatha and my son Aditya.

My dearest & closest friend R Sreedhar (who introduced me into the financial markets in 1994).

Mr. K N Ashok (who taught me the ABCD of stock markets; 1994)

Mr. K Ramesh & Mrs. Gayathri Ramesh (my first boss; Gayathri & Co. Stockbrokers; 1994-1996)

Vinod H, Ravi Kiran Acharya, A Narayan, Archie Menezes, MC Karthik, M Shakeel, Poornima Vijay, Varij Pujara, Vijayasarathy (former colleagues at Apple Stock Broking Ltd. & Apple Credit Corporation Ltd.; 1996 - 2000)

Ms. Shubra Banerjee (my boss at CCSIL - Citibank; 2000); Manoj Puravankara & Roopa (my colleagues and teammates at this bank)

Dr. Ashok Agarwal (my boss at Escorts Securities; 2000 - 2002)

Mr. Ramapriyan or fondly called as Ramu (my boss at Karvy Stock Broking Ltd. 2002 - 2010 whose unconditional support at all times inspired me to write various knowledge related material) and Anil Kumar BS, Chandrahas Devoor, V Srinivas, J Shreedhar, Manjunath BM, Muniraju CR, Major Kurian, J Venkatesh, Parthibun, Kumar, Malini Poonacha, Manohar, Basavaraj Hirur, Guruprasad, Devaraj, Jagannath AS (my former dear colleagues at the same company)

Venkatnathan sir of Karvy Debt who guided my through the learning of debt markets

Mr. Shantharam Kamath & Mr. Harindranath Shetty (former senior executives of Vijaya Bank, Head Office) and Mr. Subrat Kumar (serving senior executive at Vijaya Bank, Head Office, Bangalore)

Mrs. Beena Chotai, CFO, ICICI Venture Funds Management; Mr. Srinath Somayaji, Mr. Jayatheertha & Mr. Harshavardhan - (from the same company)

Mrs. Rajee, former VP of Canbank Venture Funds

Mr. Raja Kumar, CEO; Mr. Ajay Mittal, Director; Mr. Abhishek Loonker, Vice President (all three from Ascent Capital Advisors)

Shank Vasudev (former senior executive, Franklin Templeton Mutual Fund); Ravi Krishna (former senior executive, HSBC Mutual Fund); G Srikanth (serving senior executive, HDFC Mutual Fund); Raghunath (former senior executive, UTI Mutual Fund); Venkitesh S. Iyer (former senior executive, Franklin Templeton Mutual Fund); Mathav Kumar (serving senior executive Tata Mutual Fund); Narayan Kini (serving senior executive SBI Mutual Fund) - all are my industry friends who helped me to learn a lot of aspects of financial markets

Mrs. Ranjini Govind, Head, Property Plus supplement, The Hindu newspaper (who helped me in exploring my writing skills)

Prasad Achaiah, my dear friend and my financial advisor

Srinivasa Giri, my dear friend & inspiration behind my efforts as a writer

Dr. Chenraj Roychand Jain, Chairman, Jain Group of Institutions

Dr. Easwaran Iyer, Director & Dean, Jain College & Jain University

My dear friend and colleague Dr. Dhimant Ganatra, Associate Dean, Jain College

Prof. Hemanth Kumar, Prof. Alok Chajjer, Sanjana, Sowmya & Hema (my dear colleagues; all from Jain College)

Mr. Nishanth B, Visiting Professor, Jain College (for his kind help in formatting Excel data for this book)

Prof. N V H Krishnan, Registrar, Jain University & Prof. Lakshman Sharma, Professor, Jain University (both are responsible for my initial entry into teaching profession)

Prof. T S Ramachandran, HOD - Finance, MBA Dept. Christ University (unconditionally gave me opportunity to teach students of his college)

M/s Partridge Publishing, USA, the publishers of this book

By design and not out of desire I came to this fantastic and wonderful universe of financial services considering that I had worked in a completely different industry for seven years (1987 - 1993) before I took my baby steps in this industry in 1994. Whatever happens would happen for good and I have no regrets whatsoever has happened in my career and life. It is destiny. I have gained a lot of knowledge and more importantly a lot of knowledgeable friends and acquaintances during my course of learning. I am thankful from the bottom of my heart for those names and the respective institutions that I have mentioned above and also a lot others whose name I may not have mentioned.

The spirit to do anything is our soul and that soul belongs to God. I kneel down with respect in front of that omnipresent spirit that has guided me all these years without which I would have not reached where I have reached today. **THANK YOU GOD FOR BEING THERE ALL ALONG & GUIDING ME.**

BALAJI RAO D G

Foreword

That morning I had picked one pomegranate from a lot of four that I had purchased the previous night and started cutting it open. But I found it had rotten from inside. It was completely gone. I threw it in the dustbin with a cringe on my face. I picked the second one from the lot and cut it open; it was good and I found the rest of the pomegranates to be good too; three out of four were eatable. Then I started to pick oranges from a lot of seven. The first three were good and very tasty too. But the fourth and fifth were bad, not eatable at all; I threw them in the dustbin. The sixth and seventh were good.........

Suddenly I realized while I started cleaning the dining table that investments too were something very similar to my fruit experience. We make some investments thinking they would be good and would satisfy our investment requirements, but that may not be the case all the time. Some of the investments may not turn out to be good experience. Should I expect all my investments to be good all the time? Just like I cannot find all the fruits or vegetables to be in the same order of perfection, investments too are something like this.

Because we had a bad experience with pomegranates or oranges would we stop buying and eating them in the future? No, we would be more careful the next time. But, many times even when we think we have made some careful decisions we still may go wrong. And that is life, isn't it?

Investments in fixed deposits, equities, gold, real estate etc. are all part of such decisions we make in life. But we would be prejudiced in many circumstances. For instance, one day when my uncle came home and said that he sold a property he had bought for Rs.30 lakhs some 14 years ago for Rs.1.50 crore, everyone in our family congratulated him and also discussed about this "astonishing" growth for at least one more month. All discussions in all types of get-togethers invariably centred on the "gain" this uncle had made. Everyone who were part of the discussions had gone home with a face which said "lucky guy" and they were not as lucky.

Out of curiosity I wanted to check how much returns had my uncle made in these 14 years. I took my calculator and calculated the profit he had made in percentage and surprisingly found that the annual growth rate over these 14 years had been just 12.18%. That's it?? Barely 3 or 4 percent more than a bank deposit. But who would literally calculate and find out the real rate of returns? People are busy calculating 30 had become 150 in 14 years and concluding that it was a terrific investment.

I logged on to my laptop and fished out my research templates and found that the Sensex, the main index of Bombay Stock Exchange, which was quoting in the range of 4000 during February 2001 was 29000 fourteen years later in February 2015. The compounded returns were 15.20%!! Voila. Which meant that had the same Rs.30 lakhs were to be invested in Sensex stocks or an Index Fund and left it untouched for 14 years it would have grown to become a little over Rs.2.17 crores!! A cool 45% more profit compared to the real estate investment in the same 14 year period. But most of them get carried away with the returns given by real estate. Some numbers for us to ponder.......

Lack of financial literacy has been a bane of this country since there is no formal way of learning about such aspects because our schools/ colleges are busy teaching our kids English, science, social, algebra, economics and accounts. The outcome of such lack of exposure to financial and investment related topics has made people to shun other assets making them clinging on to real estate and gold/silver whose prices have gone through the roof because of concentrated, mindless and senseless buying. We have to change this and change this pretty quickly. The financial future for a 24 or 25 year old youth looks very bleak if he or she does not adopt an "informed" investing path.

At the current inflation of education related expenses, to educate a kid that is just born today the parents would have to spend/invest not less than Rs.62.50 lakhs (you would find such templates in this book). Where does the funds come from? Can real estate, gold/silver, chit funds do the magic?

It has taken me almost three years to complete this book. Though the number of pages are very less and may not conform to be of normal book size standards, but I can assure you it has sapped my energy to relate and create a simple reading and learning material. My job of writing this content was easier because I have been practicing the advisory concepts for a long time that I have discussed in this book through conversational mode and been successful too.

All chapters are interconnected that deals with most of the financial & investment products and has been written in simple language avoiding jargons as much as possible so that any investor/individual would understand and relate to it easily. The data enclosed in the book in MS Excel formats are all carefully compiled without any exaggerations. Needless to say this book would be a good reference material for all young and old investors who may have several doubts about investment products and confused how to deal with them. I invite readers to write to me for any clarifications, feedbacks and even criticisms.

I hope you would enjoy the reading through the conversational stories that I have weaved as much as I enjoyed writing them.

BALAJI RAO D G

Disclaimer

This book is presented as a conversational reading material with a sincere purpose of knowledge enhancement and is in any manner neither an investment advice nor is an intention towards soliciting any kind of business. The names of the stocks, prices of stocks, names of mutual funds' schemes and themes, Net Asset Values (NAVs), insurance plan names, percentages, weightages and all such numerical facts are only indicative and have been quoted only as examples. In certain cases real time stock names, stock prices, mutual fund schemes' names and themes and NAVs have been mentioned and the intention is for making the readers easy to understand the concepts. The intention in this book is not to misguide any person or organization, which is only written as an effort towards making a common lay person financial and investment literate. The writer and publisher of this material/ book specifically disclaims any liability that is incurred from the use, application or recommendation of the reports. The writer or publisher shall no way be held liable for any losses or damages, including but not limited to special, incidental, consequential, accidental or other damages. Legal, professional, tax, accounting and any other form of advice should be sought from a professional advisor or organization and is no way implied in this material. The content accuracy is not guaranteed. Readers are advised to take their own investment decisions as deemed fit by them.

Disclaimer

Reference Acknowledgements

www.moneycontrol.com

www.valueresearchonline.com

www.nseindia.com

www.bseindia.com

www.rbi.org.in

Business Line newspaper

The Hindu Newspaper

Most of the statistical figures quoted in the book have been sourced from the above websites, newspapers and magazines and I am thankful as well as grateful for them for making such information available.

Contents

-1-

BASICS OF FINANCIAL LITERACY

"Dad, I want you to buy me a gear cycle, my friend Karthik has one."

"No, Aditya, it is too expensive. I will get you next year. I can't spend that kind of money now."

"Why dad, you can go to that ATM room and withdraw money like you always do."

"Oh, I see. Where do you think the money in the ATM machine came from?"

"I don't know, dad. But I have seen you and many others going inside that room and coming out with cash."

"It is not what you think, Adi. The money there is kept by the bank and that money is what I earn by working which a bank dispenses as per my account balance."

"I am not able to understand it dad."

"See Adi, I go to work every day morning isn't it? The company that I work for pays me a salary every month for my contribution which gets deposited first week of every month into my bank. I can withdraw only such money that I earn."

"So how will you decide how much to withdraw every time you draw money from an ATM?"

"That is a good question, son. Your mom and I decide on the monthly budget that we need to make a living and the rest is treated as savings."

"What is a budget dad?"

"Budget is the total money that we need each month to make a living, such as, purchasing groceries, milk, vegetables & fruits, fuel expenses, electricity & water charges, cable TV & telephone charges, your school fees, chocolates/biscuits for you and such other expenses which can be called as Mandatory Living Expenses."

"Then what are savings?"

"The salary I bring home minus the expenses as budgeted is called as Savings."

"Which money do you withdraw from the bank then?"

"I withdraw to meet mandatory expenses of the house as also to meet some unplanned expenses."

"Unplanned expenses? What are they dad?"

"Remember last Sunday our water pipe suddenly broke and we had to get it repaired immediately for which we had to pay the plumber, it becomes an unplanned expense. Or suddenly any of us might fall sick and spend on doctor fees and medicines or you might pester me for a toy or a gadget or a cycle which makes me to withdraw additional money from the bank's ATM."

"That means now too you can withdraw money and buy me a gear cycle."

"No Adi, to do so I have to have excess funds with me which I may not have all the time to keep withdrawing. You have to understand that from the money I earn after spending I have to make some investments too from my savings."

"Investments! What is that?"

"I need to save some money by investing in certain financial assets for future requirements. For example, when you start growing up I need funds for your college admission which might run into a few lakhs. If I do not save and invest for that event then how will you go to a good college?"

"Oh, yes dad. I want to do MBA like you."

"That is a good aspiration. You know son, now you are 11 year old and ten years from now when you will be 21 years you will be ready for your post-graduation. At that time taking inflation into account I might need around Rs.12 lakhs for your MBA admission."

"So much it will cost! What is inflation dad?"

"Adi you are on a learning spree today, nevertheless, I will explain what it is. Inflation is the cost of future value of money. For example, if the cost of an item is Rs.100 today, due to various reasons the cost of the same item could become Rs.110 next year same day."

"I did not understand dad."

"See as the days passes-by the value of money reduces which can be attributed to inflation. Or the prices of goods will rise. When there is more money in the hands of people the prices rise because everyone wants to buy which naturally pushes the price of a commodity."

"I want to know more, dad."

"Okay. There are other reasons too for prices going high at a future date. When a country starts flourishing people start earning more and their affordability to purchase what they want will improve. Many times people will start splurging (spending excessively) on various items. The real price of a commodity will never be known because if a higher price is quoted and it is accepted by a few people that price will become a benchmark or a yardstick. Others who cannot afford too will have to pay the same price and naturally the prices start rising."

"Now I am beginning to understand."

"Good. These are very simple examples. But there are other bigger reasons too for the prices to rise. For example, our country do not produce oil so we import a lot from oil rich countries as we consume a lot of petrol and diesel. Our government has to pay in foreign currency to import oil and for some reason or the other the international oil prices keep raising and we have to procure it at whatever maybe the cost. Higher imports always leads to economic imbalance and also may fuel inflation if not managed well by the government. On the contrary, as witnessed during the last few months of 2014 the international oil prices dropped significantly leading to drop in domestic fuel prices. Immediately the inflation level eased. Hence, it is imperative to understand certain macro-economic factors to arrive at what drives inflation.

"You know Adi, the government has to do a lot of work to control inflation. It has to create plenty of employment opportunities so that people are able to earn and pay taxes. They also have to encourage spending which leads to collecting taxes indirectly from us. Government is not a business organisation to earn profits, the money it collects as taxes is what it spends on various developmental activities.

"Further, the government has to create good environment encouraging people to save and also invest. So it has to offer healthy savings rates through banks and post offices. The money we keep in banks will help the credit (loan) requirements of various entities such as industries to borrow and invest as capital into their businesses."

"Oh great dad, I think I learnt a lot about money today. Thank you. Get me the cycle when you can, I will not ask you till next year."

"That's good sonny, I will tell you more about money management as you grow up."

-2-

ABOUT GOVERNMENT AND THE ECONOMY

"Dad why does India always has Fiscal Deficit rather than Fiscal Surplus? How does the government manage this deficit year after year?"

"First let's know what is the meaning of Fiscal Deficit or Surplus is. These terms are derived from "Fiscal Policy" a policy which is an outcome of Annual Budget announcement by the ruling government - how much money to spend and on what to be a healthy economy and importantly how to mobilize the money to meet the expenses. Such policy announcements are termed as "fiscal policy" which is an annual affair across all economies across the world. You know Adi, to manage the finances of our country the government needs approximately Rs.18 to 20 lakh crore which is not a small amount.

"Government is like a large organization but which is not profit oriented; it has to run a country with the sole objective of economic stability. Now, how can an organization if it is a country run without money? So for that purpose the government has to collect taxes which are bifurcated as Direct Taxes & Indirect Taxes."

"Dad what are Direct & Indirect Taxes?"

"Wait Adi, I will explain. Direct Taxes are those that we pay directly to the government through Income Tax payments on our income, such as, income from salary, business, profession, rent etc. These are usually paid once a year. Even the Property Taxes that we pay on our house, if owned, comes under direct taxes. Indirect Taxes are those that are very common and are hidden in a product or a service that we purchase or avail. For example, when we buy a bathing soap for Rs.25 some component of tax is already in the price from which the manufacturer/distributor will pay the tax component by way of sales tax to the government. When we buy a movie ticket we would have paid taxes indirectly by way of entertainment tax to the government. Service Tax, Sales Tax, Custom Duty are all examples of indirect taxes."

"Okay dad, it is now clear. Every year you pay tax on your income to the IT department is part of direct tax collection by the government, isn't it?"

"Absolutely. Continuing understanding fiscal deficit, as I said earlier government has to run this country for which it needs funds and loads of funds. For example, during a financial year from April to March let's say government has a total funds requirement of Rs.100; to meet this requirement government has to collect money by way of direct & indirect taxes; despite its efforts if government is able to collect only Rs.50 out of the required Rs.100 there will be a deficit of Rs.50. This will lead to fiscal deficit or budget deficit."

"Oh, then what will government do to meet this shortfall?"

"That is when government starts its borrowing program. The government starts borrowing from internal sources, raising funds from domestic resources such as by issuing Treasury Bills for short term maturities that mature under one year and also issue long term securities termed as G-Sec or Govt. Securities of maturities ranging from 2 years to 30 years which are subscribed by those who have surplus-investable money such as individuals, corporates and institutions. For example, the Provident Fund or PF that a salaried employee contributes gets invested in such Government Securities is part of the government's borrowing. Further, by way of issuing of post office savings certificates such as National Saving Certificate (NSC), Kisan Vikas Patra (KVP), Public Provident Fund (PPF), Monthly Investment Scheme (MIS) and others government borrows funds and if that too is not enough then it resorts to borrowing from other countries such as International Monetary Fund, Asian Development Bank and other such institutions. All these borrowing further put pressure on the government because it has to service the interest payments."

"Any other solutions to cut down on the borrowings dad?"

"Yes there are. Disinvestments are another method to reduce such borrowings or to meet the budget deficit."

"What is disinvestment?"

"Over a period of time government would have invested in setting up various businesses by way of corporations. For example, Hindustan Petroleum, Bharat Petroleum, Indian Oil Corp, ONGC, Steel Authority of India, National Thermal Power Corp, Coal India, Bharat Heavy Electricals, Bharat Electronics, National Hydro Power Corp, Maruti Udyog (Now Maruti Suzuki), Engineers India and such other Public Sector Undertakings (PSUs) were investments done by the government long ago which it decides to sell a part of its stake or ownership to new investors such as to general public that includes small (retail), large (individuals & corporates with large amounts of investable funds) and institutional investors through the process of a public issue. When the government decides to offload or sell its equity or ownership to new investors they are termed as Disinvestment, also called as Offer for Sale (OFS). Over the last 15 - 20 years government has divested from many such companies that has helped the government to mop-up over $30 billion, equivalent to about one lakh eighty thousand crore in Indian rupee. Such programs have given the required stimulus for the government to borrow less that reduces the interest burden."

"Very interesting dad."

"Of course, the financial system itself is very fascinating to understand. What you also have to understand is that when you start earning you should pay your taxes on time and disclose all your income properly and pay all the taxes. The more we try to avoid paying taxes the more burden it will be on the government to maintain economic stability. As reported by Business Line in its newspaper dated 07th Feb 2015 a country of 120 crore population only 3.50 crore people pay taxes which is a cause of concern."

"Oh really sad, that is the reason why Income Tax department keeps advertising in the newspapers requesting all income earners to pay taxes without evading it."

"Yes. It is our duty to pay taxes and pay as per our slab. If we evade taxes the burden is not on the government it is in fact burdening the country itself of which we are the citizens. Since government is not a profit-motive entity it will pass-on such burdens to the citizens indirectly which we may not see directly. We all have to be aware of this."

"Super dad, I learnt a lot more than I actually wanted to know."

"Sure, learning is a continuous process son."

-3-

WHY SHOULD YOU START EARLY TO INVEST?

India was playing against Australia in a one day match. India needed 100 runs in the remaining 10 overs to win the match at 10 runs per over and they were seemed to be struggling with the required rate. Now grown up and employed 24 year old Aditya (fondly called by his family & friends as Adi) who was watching the match with his father had been tensed for a while because India had to score 5 runs per over at the beginning of the match and now in the 41st over they had put themselves in a mess of having to score 10 runs per over with just 4 wickets left to win the all-important match. Aditya made an exasperated comment as to why didn't the batsmen start scoring at a planned pace of 5 runs per over when they had adequate time for such planning from the first over. His father who was not as tensed as his son said, "You know Adi, real life too is like a one day cricket match. If you have to plan yourself to have adequate money by the time you are 50 years, you should start early in life, as early as 25 years, not start when you are 35 years."

Moving his beanbag closer to his father Adi asked inquisitively, "Why do you say like that, dad?" His father continued, "For example, if the current monthly household expenses is Rs.15000, then at an annual inflation growth rate of 6% by the time you are 50 years, that is 26 years from today, you would need approximately Rs.68000 per month to meet the same Rs.15000 worth of expenses. That's inflation for you. And if you are planning to retire at 50 years of age, you would need about Rs.2.00 crore as your retirement corpus."

Adi jumped from his seat asking, "Wow dad, so much money, why would I need that much funds at my age of 50 years, I think it is too much."

"It is quite simple, son. Understand this fact first. In the year 1995-96 the bank fixed deposit rate was around 15% p.a. while the rate of interest now in 2014-15 is in the range of 8% to 9% p.a. What makes you think that the bank interest rate will remain to be higher than this in the future? Check the current interest rates of the developed countries and you will find good reasons to believe that the interest rates will drop to considerably low levels some 10 or 20 years from now. It is economics which I shall explain to you some other time. My gut feeling is that the interest rate 25 years from today would be less than 4% p.a. and not trying to scare you let's assume it as 4%. But back to why would you need Rs.2.00 crores when you are 50 years. When you get older your risk taking ability would also change, so...."

Adi interrupted, "why, dad, will my risk profile change as I age? I think I will continue to be aggressive all my life."

Father asked him, "Tell me what speed you ride your bike and what speed I ride?"

Adi said, "I ride at least 80 kms. / hour speed and you ride too slow dad. I think you are pretty conservative in your approach."

His father laughed and said, "Don't forget son, I too have crossed your age and become 55 years now. When I was your age I too was riding my bike at high speed, as I am aging I have slowed down or rather mellowed down. I guarantee you that as you age your speed too will subside significantly; it is the rule of life. So, don't bet on being aggressive all your life. Same is the case with risk profile. As we age our risk taking ability too will reduce and we invariably look at safer investment options. When you turn 50 years you will quite naturally invest your retirement funds in a bank to get regular monthly income to sustain your mandatory expenses. If you have created a corpus of Rs.2.00 crore, at 4% p.a. interest rate the bank will give you Rs.8 lakhs per annum as interest and if you divide it by 12 months you will be able to withdraw

Rs.67000 per month to meet your monthly expenses. Now do you realize why would you need Rs.2.00 crores as your retirement corpus?"

"Dad you could be right. But how on earth can I manage to create such a humongous corpus in 25-26 years?" The young man seemed alarmed of the figure.

"Rome was not built in a day son. You can plan for your retirement corpus from this first month of receiving your salary itself. You are starting to work from next month isn't it? I guess your salary would be Rs.35000 a month?"

"Yes dad. But I will get about Rs.31000 in hand."

"That's because you have to pay certain taxes on your income and your company deducts towards provident fund or PF that again is a saving. But I have noticed you are spending too much money on gadgets, eating out, gifting and splurging money on many unwanted things. Instead, if you start investing Rs.10000 a month in opportunities that can offer about 12% to 15% annual compounded returns over the next 26 years you can create a corpus in excess of Rs.2.00 crore. With a good asset allocation mix across debt, equity and gold I am confident that you could achieve this kind of returns."

India now needed 12 runs per over in the remaining 5 overs to win the match. But Adi was more interested in the life's run rate than of the match and was intently listening to his father, whom he knew was a meticulous planner.

"See son, to achieve the same target of Rs.2 crore if you start investing when you are 30 years you would need to invest Rs.20000 each month and if you start at 35 years you would need Rs.40000 a month. The decision is yours."

"Really dad, I never realised this. Indeed, real life too is like a one day cricket match. Would you tell me how to achieve 12% or 15% compounded returns over the next 25 - 26 years? Because I feel achieving this is difficult."

"It is neither difficult nor improbable. I will explain another day not today as I have to check a few aspects before I tell you how. See India need to score 30 runs in 12 balls with 2 wickets left. I am not watching the match." He got up from his chair and walked towards his room.

"Me too, the situation is hopeless and thanks for your advice dad." Aditya turned the TV off.

"You are welcome, son."

-4-

HOW YOU CAN AVOID TAKING AN EDUCATION LOAN?

Aditya's face was tensed when he returned home from work that evening. His mother, worried, asked for the reason but he didn't say anything convincingly and went straight inside his room. She waited for her husband to come home from his walk and told him about Adi. His father knocked on his son's room door, walked in asking, "How was the day, son? I heard from your mother that you weren't feeling too well. What's the matter? Is everything okay?"

Adi said, "Nothing dad. Arun is yet to find a job and he is in stress to start repaying his education loan. The bank has been reminding him regularly about commencement of his repayment. He is clueless what to do. He has been trying hard to find a job but somehow it is not happening. I feel helpless."

His father knew how close they both were since their pre-university days. Adi asked his father, "How did you manage to pay for my MBA admission, dad, without taking a loan? I never asked you this question before & why did Arun's father had to take a loan? They are not poor either."

"Look son, poorness is not about money alone, it can be about poor planning. I know Arun can ask his father to pay until he finds a job, but he does not want to pass that pressure on to his father. The situation is delicate and rather emotional between Arun and his father."

"Yes, dad, you are right. That's the reason Arun is stressed out."

"You asked as to how I managed to pay the full amount of Rs.5.50 lakhs for your MBA admission. It was a simple planning that I did when you were 11 year old."

"Dad, you planned for my education when I was just 11 years?" Adi asked incredulously.

"Of course, I did. You would be even more surprised if I tell you I invested just Rs.2000 every month for 10 years and created a corpus of Rs.5 lakhs. In fact, by the time you completed your graduation I was ready with the money."

"What are you saying dad? Just Rs.2000 a month and you created my MBA admission corpus?"

"Does it sound unbelievable? That is the power of planning you see. You getting into a professional course was a "foreseen event" for me when you were about 11 year old and given my savings capacity then I could afford to save and invest only for an MBA course than for engineering or medicine. Every drop of water creates an ocean and those small amounts invested without a break helped me create the required corpus."

"Wow, dad that was a great thinking from you."

"We might fail in our planning, but we should never fail to plan and implement. For your post- graduation purpose I invested Rs.1000 p.m. in post office Recurring Deposit and Rs.1000 p.m. through a Systematic Investment Plan approach in a diversified equity mutual fund every month for 10 years which gave me compounded returns of little more than 12% which helped me in creating a corpus of Rs.5.00 lakhs for your admission. You were able to join a prestigious college as well, didn't you?"

"I feel sad for Arun. Had his father been a little more thoughtful probably he would have not had to go through the current predicament and stress. The biggest moral dad is that we tend to complicate simple things."

"The power of compounding was called as the 8th wonder of the world by none other than Albert Einstein. The effect of compounding is more effective over longer periods of time and adding equity into such long term planning can yield amazing returns. In fact, for all foreseen events we can plan well in advance. Only glitch is that we do not do it systematically."

"Now come, let's have some coffee, you still look tired." Aditya's dad concluded the conversation.

-5-

IMPORTANCE OF FINANCIAL PLANNING

"Congratulations and best wishes son on your first month salary. So what are your plans of how you would like to use your money?"

"Thanks dad. I am really excited to see my bank account credited with my first salary; my first hard-earned money! But I have not decided on anything as yet. First I would like to give you all a party and celebrate."

"That's great, it is indeed time to celebrate. The first earning is always special."

"But dad, how should I plan my expenses & savings? Please advise me."

"Sure I will. Your salary is Rs.35000 p.m. isn't it?

"Yes dad, they are doing some deductions. About Rs.31000 and odd are at my disposal."

"Yeah, provident fund contributions from you and your employer helps you in creating a good corpus in long term which offers assured returns as well. The rest of the planning have to be done from this month itself."

"But I am not even 25 years old dad, should I start so early? Can't I wait for another couple of years and then start?"

"No, no, no Adi, you have mistaken. It is imperative that you do not waste any time by procrastinating. Let me tell you a few facts of managing finances and investing habits. Remember I had told you that life is like a 50 over cricket match which we invariably chase; each year delay would put pressure on our building the desired amounts for the future needs."

"Yes dad, I remember."

"See, in life we go through two types of main events (a) Foreseen Events (b) Unforeseen Events. Foreseen events are (i) buying a house (ii) buying a car (iii) vacations (iv) having a family or getting married (v) once married the new responsibilities follow such as children and eventually expenses related to their upbringing & education (vii) retirement (viii) unplanned expenses

"Next and most important are Unforeseen Events such as (i) untimely or premature death (ii) loss of job (iii) long-term illness or medical conditions leading to income loss (iii) temporary or permanent disability leading to lesser income. So, life is full of events; many are foreseen a few would be unforeseen."

"I guess I will have to first look into unforeseen events and then focus on foreseen events. Right dad?"

"Smart you are son, yes, you have to first cover your unforeseen events because such events lead us to great financial losses. To meet such financial losses you will have to take the assistance of insurance companies. Insurance acts as hedge against unforeseen events which means it provides an opportunity to address financial risk arising out of accidents or unplanned events which an insurance company would compensate since we would have purchased a policy from them."

"Yes dad, I have learnt during my MBA in financial planning subject. But could you please tell me more about it?"

"When you take a loan from a bank they usually ask for a guarantor, here the idea of taking a guarantor is to ensure that in case the borrower would be unable to repay the loan they can ask the guarantor to clear it. The bank is simply "insuring" itself against a possible default by the borrower which could lead to financial losses to the lender (the bank). In insurance too the concept is very similar. We can insure ourselves against a possible financial loss occurring out of various unplanned reasons and taking the help of an insurance company by paying premiums and making them liable to compensate the loss. Just like we buy an insurance for our vehicle".

"Your example is very simple to understand dad. It is now clear why I would need an insurance. I think I will have to buy insurances to cover my premature death, health hazards and similar such possibilities".

"You are absolutely right, Adi. You will have to first cover your unforeseen events in life by buying certain insurance policies and simultaneously you should start planning for your foreseen events as I already mentioned."

"So dad, how should I begin?"

"First you buy a health insurance for Rs.5.00 lakh sum assured. I will disconnect you from my family health cover and you can start on your own to pay the premiums from this year onwards. Next, you buy a term assurance plan to cover any untimely death and for the time being these insurances are enough. Along with these you will have to start investing in various financial instruments such as debt, equity, metal and real estate to meet your foreseen events. You have to also start thinking from now about your retirement funds as well."

"Alright dad. I will first work on my financial status and then come back to you for more advice."

"Yes Adi, you do that. But do not waste time in decision making. Idle money is dead money."

"Sure dad. Will do that and thank you for your valuable advice."

-6-

WHY DEMAT?

"Adi, I had told you to open the demat account and broking account, did you open?"

"Yes dad, I finished all the documentation process yesterday and awaiting my account to get operational. They took from me my passport size photographs, PAN card copy, address proof and bank passbook updates and made me sign some member-client agreement form. Dad, I was wondering why bank passbook copies?"

"See son, the idea of asking you to submit the first set of documents you mentioned is to establish your identity along with your source of income proof through seeking PAN information. The market regulator SEBI is ensuring that the person who transacts in the stock market is genuine and he has a formal and organized source of income. Further, the bank passbook is to ensure that you have a regular flow of financial transactions, since to participate in stock markets it requires some amount of money to invest. Also in due course of your transactions with the stockbroker you will be making payments and also receiving payments to and from them so they need to know such information as part of trying to establish a fair picture of you and your financial transactions. The stockbroker would register your bank account details in their records and all future pay-outs by way of funds would get directly credited to the bank account that you have registered. This saves a lot of time and also is quite convenient."

"Oh great dad, technology can be a boon. And dad, what is this demat account? They also asked me to give the details of nominee and I have mentioned your name there. Can you please explain?"

"Like you just said technology can be a boon, the market regulator SEBI introduced demat by doing away with transacting in stocks by way of physical certificates which were in use till about 10 - 15 years ago. Physical mode of transacting was very cumbersome, time consuming and old-fashioned and had started to drive investors away from participating in the stock markets. The market regulator introduced dematerialized method of dealing which gave way to electronic mode of transacting. In simple terms, when you invest through an initial public offer or an IPO, you just mention your demat account number and if the shares are allotted to you it is credited to your account directly with an intimation of such credits. And after you start dealing with a stockbroker in the secondary market for regular buying and selling of shares the same demat account would be used to credit and debit your account with shares.

"Electronic mode of receiving and delivering shares are just like a bank account where you may not see the money physically but it gets credited or debited and you only receive an acknowledgement of such credits and debits; you are given a passbook entry to prove such incoming and outgoing amounts. Demat accounts are very similar to this. Once you open a demat account you are issued a demat holding statement which gives you all the information about such holdings and also you may demand for a transaction summary just like a passbook which gives you precise information of all stocks credited to your account and debited from your account with date and quantity."

"Cool dad, sounds pretty efficient way of dealing in the stock markets. Am I allowed to open only one demat account or can I open as many accounts?"

"No, like there are no restrictions to open any number of bank accounts you are free to open and operate as many demat accounts, but with different depository participants or DPs. Depository participants are those who are authorized by SEBI to maintain the records of the demat account holders and also offer related services. For example, Karvy, Kotak, Motilal Oswal, HDFC Bank, State Bank are all DPs who facilitate such account openings. Also you should know that above the DPs there are Depositories."

"Wow it looks like a structure of SEBI, Depositories, Depository Participants and Demat account holders"

"Yes indeed, it is a structure. Depositories are those who actually hold the securities of the demat account holders while the DPs are just who maintain the records by debiting or crediting the account as and when such transactions take place."

"Dad does that mean Depositories are very important part of this structure?"

"Of course. We have two Depositories in India - NSDL and CDSL (National Securities Depository Ltd. and Central Depository Services Ltd) which regulate the DPs. These depositories are regulated by SEBI for the simple reason that the securities have to be maintained and protected safely without any chance of misusing them. Hence, the DPs only act as facilitators while depositories hold the securities of the demat account holders."

"And dad, with whom should I ideally open a demat account - with a stockbroker or a bank?"

"From my personal experience I would say it would be ideal if you open a demat account with the stockbroker where you propose to transact for your buying and selling of shares. It would be more convenient and also your broker would be one point contact for any queries or grievances relating to your transactions both pertaining to buying and selling as also demat related. There is no point in opening a demat account with some entity where you may not regularly transact. It would be waste of money and time. Best option is to open with your active broker."

"Got it dad. And lastly, why is this nominee details taken?"

"Life is full of uncertainties. In case the account holder dies the securities that would be in the demat account could be transferred to the nominee without any problem is the reason behind such process."

"Okay, okay. And dad are there any charges that I need to incur to manage my demat account?"

"Yes, may be a small amount of money which could be in the range of Rs.500 per year, that's all. Even to open a broking account with a broker you need not have to pay anything, it comes free of cost"

"But dad, the stockbroker asked me to deposit some money with him along with opening my account. Why is this amount to be deposited? Is it his charges or something?"

"No Adi, like I just mentioned broking accounts are usually offered free of cost. The broker asked you to "deposit" certain amount of money which will be credited to your account and remains there to facilitate your future buying of stocks. Moreover, just by opening an account the broker is not gaining anything, in fact, it will be a loss for him for the money he would have spent on agreement, stamp paper charges etc. By asking you to deposit some money he is trying to ensure that you would do some transactions with him of buying and selling which would result in brokerage income for him. He is just trying to induce you to transact because the purpose of the existence of a stockbroker is to earn brokerages."

"Now I understood dad. I shall pay him an amount of Rs.5000 and he said that amount is fine."

"Yeah you do that."

"Dad, after the account gets opened I shall consult you on how to proceed."

"Sure, let me know, we will discuss on that."

-7-

BASICS OF EQUITY & INVESTING IN PUBLIC ISSUES

"Adi, there is a public issue that is opening tomorrow, why don't you invest?"

"Public issue, you mean Initial Public Offer?"

"Yes, an engineering company is offering fresh equity to fund their expansion. I did go through their offer document briefly and found their prospects pretty good. They have a good business track record, flourishing business and the future of the company looks exciting."

"But dad isn't investing in a new company risky? I don't think I should invest my hard earned money in some unknown company."

"Listen son, this life is all about risks. In fact, the foundation of our living or existence itself is fraught with number of risks and variety of vulnerabilities; it is just that we do not acknowledge it. But at least we have to take calculated risks. Investing in a new company may not be as much risk as you perceive it to be."

"Can you explain this aspect dad?"

"I am sure you have heard of companies such as Reliance Industries, Infosys, Wipro, Tata Steel, Cipla, L & T, Bajaj Motors, Havells, Jindal Steel, Mahindra & Mahindra, HDFC, Yes Bank and others. Today these companies have become top of the mind recall for all of us. But before these companies became what they are today they too were new and were looking to build successful businesses. To commence a business everyone does not like to borrow money which is actually a burden in terms of repaying the loan as also servicing interest for a long period of time. That is the reason they seek "risk-capital" which is termed as equity which in turn means sharing the ownership of the company."

"I recall that I learnt this during my MBA dad."

"Of course you would have, but let me refresh your memory. Equity is the opposite of debt. While debt does not give you the ownership rights, equity offers you ownership. While you get paid only a predefined interest on your lending in case of debt, you get a share in the profits by way of dividends in case of equity. While debt is lending, equity is an investment. In debt you are not part of the profit or losses, but in equity you are part of both profits as well as losses."

"Does that mean in debt I am not part of the profits at all if the company flourishes with my lending?"

"Absolutely no, since the promoter/company is obligated to return the capital irrespective whether his business flourishes or not why will the company make you part of the profits? Since the lender is not part of the losses in case the company does not flourish why would he be considered for the profits?"

"Then is there any guarantee that the company will flourish and will make profits that will be shared with the equity investor?"

"Let me explain this question of yours with a simple example. You are today 25 years, well educated, working and earning; which means you have flourished, isn't it?"

"Yes dad thanks to you for making me to reach where I am today. If not for you I would not have flourished."

"Great, I am glad that you acknowledged that! Over the last many years I have invested quite a bit of my hard earned money on your education, on your wellbeing and taken care of your many needs which today fortunately have yielded the desired results. Had you not done well in your studies as well as in your life my investment would have actually become an expense which would not have yielded any returns on my investment."

"Oh dad, your example is spot-on"!

"Indeed it is. My investment on you to bear the desired results I had to wait for over 20 years, which I am sure, is pretty long term. Similarly companies or promoters too will need adequate time to build their empires or businesses to offer such favourable returns on the investments."

"Very true dad."

"Every promoter, well at least most of them, dreams of building successful businesses for which they need capital and importantly they seek such capital that people invest in their ventures that is given as risk-capital because only such capital can make the promoters be aggressive with their plans and can take the required decisions to move ahead towards success. If they have a nagging problem such as to return the money within a stipulated time and keep servicing interest payments it bogs them down and may affect their performances."

"Does that mean one should invest with long term in mind?"

"Yes, it is pretty obvious that to set up a large business it takes time and sometimes it takes a very long time. Tatas, Birlas, Ambanis, Ruias, Bajajs, Nandas, Parekhs and other such illustrious names did not build such successful empires overnight, it has taken considerable period of time. Had they not taken such risks I wonder where our country be today! Reliance, Infosys, Wipro, TCS, Ranbaxy, Cipla, HDFC and many other companies are all legendary in terms of what they have offered by way of immense wealth creation and goodwill to our country."

"Yes dad, you are right."

"Adi, to invest in a company as an equity investor you need not have to risk with all your savings. Even if you consider just 20% of your savings to invest in risky investments it would help you create long term wealth. Generally people do not take the asset allocation route of investing and tend to have a concentrated investment portfolio."

"Dad, what is concentrated investment portfolio?"

"Many people buy a lot of real estate or buy a lot of gold & silver or even invest heavily in bank deposits. While real estate is not easy to liquidate and also is not tax friendly, gold cannot be considered as a real investment since it does not offer any returns and is as volatile as equity instruments. And you know that fixed deposit type of investment offer only a fixed return and again is not tax friendly."

"What about equity investments dad, are they easy to liquidate and tax friendly?"

"The best aspect about equity is they are easy to liquidate and also very tax friendly. If you buy stocks you can sell on a stock exchange and get your money in exactly 3 days and if you are investing in an equity mutual fund then you would get your money in exactly 4 days. Also the short term capital gains are taxed at 15% and long term capital gains are completely tax free along with any dividends earned which too are exempt from any type of taxes."

"Wow dad, it sounds very good. Why is that equity has been given such good tax status?"

"Wait son, don't jump into conclusions. While equity is good on liquidity and tax friendly it is not an assured product. The returns depend upon the performance of the company over a longer period of time. If you are able to pick fundamentally sound companies the chances of losing your investment would be considerably very less. And why it has been made tax friendly is that the government is compensating for the risk being taken by the investor. For example, real estate is low to moderate on risk as an investment that is why for the first three years the profits are taxed as per the tax slab of the individual which can go up to 30%. In case of gold and silver again the risk is moderate so the short term capital gains are taxed on three year basis which is as per the tax slab of the individual and on fixed deposit type of fixed income instrument there is neither long term nor short term, all gains are taxed as per the individual tax status. The reason is - the risk taken on real estate, gold and fixed deposit are far less compared to equity hence the risk being taken is compensated by way of making it tax-friendly. Moreover, it motivates people to take risk."

"Awesome dad. The logic is quite good."

"Now you should consider investing in this engineering company's IPO. As a market regulator SEBI has made it mandatory for all companies who want to raise money through the public issue route to follow very strict procedures such as engaging a merchant banker/underwriter, preparing offer documents and such other formalities as also all the issues are to obtain a IPO grading from reputed rating agencies such as CRISIL, CARE or ICRA which offers an easy understanding of the quality of the issue." (The grading now is made optional for companies)

"Okay dad, I will surely invest. I had never understood the actual difference between risk capital & risk-free capital. Now I am clear about it."

"Finally note that every investment has inherent risks. You should not pin your hopes on one investment to give you the desired returns. Businesses do fail despite best laid plans, it is part of life. Hence, it would be imperative to diversify your risks by investing in different companies and businesses. You make some good decisions and some bad ones; take it in your stride. Let not one bad investment deter you from not investing at all. There is no such thing as perfection in life. You are young and I am sure you can absorb some risks over a longer period of time."

"Thanks dad, I hope this company does well."

"Also remember before you choose to invest in a public issue do understand the company's strengths and weaknesses. If you cannot read and understand from the issuing company's offer document then read some recommendations which are done by some analysts and stockbrokers that would be available easily on the net and in newspapers. Make a good judgement before investing."

"Dad, is there a guarantee that I would have got all the number of shares that I had applied for?"

"No, no. There are no such guarantees or assurances. It all depends upon the subscription that the company receives for their public offer. Many times they receive more money than they had planned to raise which leads to "Over Subscription". For example, a company may had wanted to raise Rs.100 crore, but they receive Rs.200 crore or even Rs.500 crore making it 2 times or 5 times over-subscribed. Obviously under this situation the company cannot allot shares to everyone, hence it would be done on "proportionate basis" (pro-rata). If you had applied for 100 shares and the issue got 5 times subscribed then you could be allotted just 20 shares.

Another type is "fully subscribed" which means the company received the full IPO money leading to allotting full shares. Had you applied for 100 shares, under fully subscribed possibility, you could be allotted the entire 100 shares applied by you.

The last possibility is "under-subscription" which means the company fails to receive the entire money that it had planned for; in India if the company does not receive at least 90% of the total equity that was planned to raise the company may cancel the issue (there are other underwriting concepts which could be learnt separately)."

"Wow, so much about a public issue dad!"

"Yes son. There are so many other aspects as well. But from a working knowledge point of view this much is enough to understand. Because many people do not know the reason behind not getting full allotments or why their monies got refunded, hence I explained this briefly."

"Understood dad. Lastly, after the IPO process the shares will be listed on stock exchanges, isn't it?"

"Yes of course. The shares that are issued through public issue (IPO) route would definitely get listed on recognized stock exchanges, NSE and/or BSE. The listing is facilitated so as to get a market driven price for the shares that you would have been allotted by the company. The shares, if it were to be allotted, would be credited to your demat account which you can sell after listing. And there is no specific rule as to when you should sell; you can sell whenever you feel it is worth selling. Selling on the listing day too can be considered if the price on that day offers satisfactory returns on your investment. Such decisions can be made by the investor as per his or her choice. To facilitate such buying and selling opportunities on a continuous basis "secondary market" by way of stock exchanges have been established."

"Got it dad. I go to know a lot about new issues."

"We will learn more in the days to come son."

-8-

BASICS OF ASSET ALLOCATION

"Adi, since your account now with the stockbroker will be opened shortly, why don't you start buying some good stocks in small quantities?"

"No dad. I am still thinking."

"What is there to think? Your broker offers you so many recommendations of which stocks to buy and what rate to buy, check them out and start placing the orders in small numbers."

"Not that dad, I am thinking whether it is worth to risk my hard-earned money since equities are risky by nature."

"Oh come on, son. Don't be a sissy. I have told you on several occasions that risk is part of our lives, why are you worried so much? A little bit of risk does not kill you. And moreover given the current inflationary trend and the number of financial goals to be achieved you have to take some risk otherwise you will never be able to have enough when you grow older."

"Dad, are you scaring me?"

"Why should I? Listen carefully, everyone earns their money the hardest way; it is not only you who has hard earned money. You only have to make prudent investment decisions that's all."

"How to decide dad?"

"What is the current inflation levels in 2014-15?"

"I remember reading it in the newspapers as around 8%. Am I right?"

"Yes, see the good habits of reading newspapers! Now what has been the one year bank fixed deposit rates over the last one year?"

"I guess it is in the range of 8.50% to 9% p.a."

"You are right again. For example, had you invested Rs.100 last year same day in a bank FD at the rate of 9%, today the FD would have matured and you withdraw your principal along with interest of Rs.109, right?"

"Yea dad, I will have Rs.109 with me."

"What is the inflation currently you said? It is 8%, na? On the interest income that you earned you are supposed to pay income tax and even if you are in the lowest tax bracket you still would have to pay 10% which makes your net income 8.10% after taxes, are you following?"

"Oh dad, I had forgotten about the tax obligation."

"But still you are obligated to pay, ignorance is not bliss. With inflation at 8% and your post tax returns is 8.10% what is your real rate of return? It is 0.10%, are you happy with the returns?"

"No dad, how can I be happy with such paltry returns?"

"Now if you are not happy with 0.10% return how will you beat the monster called "inflation"?

"How dad, I am being clueless."

"Don't act naïve. You have to obviously take risk with your investments. Your continuous endeavour is to invest in such opportunities that offer you inflation beating returns. At least you should be able to generate 4% to 5% additional returns compared to inflation, only then you can overcome the negative effects of inflation."

"So should I start investing in those stocks suggested by you?"

"I am not coercing or forcing you into investing in stocks or equities. I am just trying to offer you a perspective on why you should start considering risk as part of your investment plans. The risk you take should be well researched and you should monitor your investments regularly. It also does not mean that you should invest all your savings in risky assets."

"Then how should I begin dad?"

"It is ideal if you follow "asset allocation" based investing. For example, if your savings ability after expenses and commitments is Rs.5000 per month, then allocate this surplus in this manner: Rs.1500 into fixed income instruments such as bank deposits or recurring deposits that are risk free, Rs.500 into gold through gold mutual funds that is considered to be moderate on risk and balance Rs.3000 into equities that is of high risk. Since you are young higher exposure to risky assets may not hurt you much. Such asset allocation based investing will help you in diversifying risk as also will offer you an equilibrium of returns. The collective returns could easily help you in overcoming inflation."

"This sounds good dad, I was thinking I should invest all my savings in equity. Now I am clear. I will surely follow your advice of investing in different assets. Thank you dad for clarifying the doubts"

"Anytime son, but do not delay in beginning your investments. Sooner the better."

-9-

DIFFERENCE BETWEEN TRADING & INVESTING

"Dad, I have received a confirmation from the stockbroker who has given me my demat account number and my client ID, I will finally start trading in the stock markets!"

"Hold on son, what is this you are saying that you will start trading?"

"Yes dad the broker said my trading account is now open and he said I am ready to trade. So I will be starting to trade. Is there a problem with that?"

"No, there is no problem. But I was wondering if you are getting confused with the terms "trading" and "investing."

"I thought both terms were same. Is there any difference dad?"

"Of course, both these terms are hugely different from one another. It has become a normal practice to use the term "trading" even though one may not trade at all."

"Dad, could you please be more specific, perhaps, with some examples."

"Okay listen, stock market is a place of opportunities. Such opportunities would open up once you decide how you want to use it for your benefit. For example, if a recommendation is given to you that ITC as a stock whose current market price (CMP) is Rs.350 could touch Rs.355 before 3.30 today this would be an Intraday Trading Call which means you can buy ITC shares at Rs.350 and expect to sell it at Rs.355 before the market closes today (market operates from 9.15 am to 3.30 pm, Monday to Friday). And if the same call is given saying that ITC could touch Rs.400 a year from today and if you buy with that expectation, it is called as Delivery Call and you may have to wait for a year for the prediction to come true. This example defines if you like to be a Trader or an Investor."

"Well dad. Are these predictions guaranteed? Will such targets be achieved in the given time frame?"

"No, no Adi, all predictions come with a Terms & Conditions apply clause, which is to cut your losses by applying what is termed as "stop loss" if the prediction has started to go against your favour. For example, if you have purchased ITC on an "intraday" basis (buying & selling in the same trading day) at Rs.350 with a target of Rs.355 and if the price starts coming down instead of going up, you can choose the option of selling and getting out of the position below the purchase price; may be at Rs.347. Which means, if the price of ITC starts coming down instead of going up as predicted, when it reaches Rs.347 you would actually exit the position by booking a loss of Rs.3 per share which potentially protects you from huge losses if the price had fallen beyond expectations."

"Dad, does that mean that all targets given as recommendations may or may not come true?"

"Absolutely, the problem with speculative trades are that the price can go either way pretty quickly depending upon the position held by you which could eat into your investments. So be careful what you choose to do in the market – do you want to trade which also means you are speculating or do you want to invest?"

"Dad, I am confused actually. But trading sounds exciting."

"Yes indeed trading can be exciting and very risky as well. It is like riding a tiger; it would be exciting, but you should know how to control and manage it. If you propose to earn a small amount of money daily or weekly on any stock then you are speculating which also means you do not want to own the stock, but you are just speculating on the price movement; this is just the opposite of investing."

"Okay, should I choose to be a trader or investor dad?"

"That is a very tricky question. It all depends on what do you expect from the stock market. If you desire to earn short term profits and also prepared to incur losses then you need to be very active by continuously looking at the markets, prices and other technical charts which could eat into your productive time. Further, if you are capable of understanding the dynamics of various analysis and also capable of withstanding the losses you can choose to be a trader. Remember, being trader is hard work. Unless you do not have continuous focus and able to track the price and volume movements you may not be a successful trader. You may make money but only out of fluke. And also you may need large amounts of money which is required to be paid as margins to the stockbroker who would adjust such margins in case you incur losses and in certain circumstances you could lose the entire margin and more. The choice is yours."

"Sounds tough. But are you discouraging me dad?"

"May be I am. Somehow I am not a big fan of speculative trades. Having a trading mind set is like having an affair while investing for long term in stocks is like getting married. I have preferred the latter always. Since trading has several inherent risks associated with it you should tread the path very carefully."

"That is a nice example dad. I think I too would like to invest rather than trade, what do you say?"

"Good decision I guess. At least you do not have to invest your time constantly to track the market or the prices of the stocks. Investing on the contrary does not require so much of time. Fundamental Research reports would offer you a fair understanding of the company's financials, macro-economic situation and prospects, sector related pros & cons and the stock specific information. So you can choose fundamentally good companies and start accumulating at different price levels which could offer you dividends that are tax-free, bonuses and also may offer you handsome capital appreciation in the long term. In my personal experience of over 20 years of investing in stocks though I have incurred losses investing in some companies, largely I have gained and have no regrets whatsoever. When I am taking risk I have always been ready to lose in some and win from some. Overall my investing balance sheet shows I have not lost and even achieved an inflation beating returns. I am happy with that outcome."

"Alright dad. I understood the difference between trading and investing. I think I too will stick to investing method rather than trading."

"That's nice. Also note that for traders they follow what is termed as Technical Analysis that tracks the price and volume pattern of stocks and this type of analysis claims to have the ability to predict the price outcome of the stock in the future. There are several technical analysts who churn out such reports each day and meet the trading requirements of several speculators/traders. And for investors they follow what is termed as Fundamental Analysis that tracks the fundamentals of a company such as quantitative and qualitative factors that may influence the company's performance in the future."

"Yes dad, I think I have learnt these in my MBA."

"Yeah they have such subjects at the MBA level. Traders prefer technical analysis and investors prefer fundamental analysis and both these analysis are important for the market and its various participants including fund managers and portfolio managers."

"Great dad. I understood it clearly. And are there are charges that I have to pay for transacting with the stockbroker?"

"Oh, I forgot to mention about the charges. Since a stockbroker is a facilitator to buy and sell shares he charges what is termed as "brokerage" which is actually a commission for rendering such service. As per the SEBI rule the brokerages charged by any stockbroker should not exceed 2.50% of the contract value. But now the space has become very competitive and the brokerages have come down to as low as 0.25% to 0.50% of the contract value for delivery based trades. And further there would be some small levies such as securities transaction tax, service tax, stamp duty etc. which would be added. These information would be provided by your stockbroker when you are opening your account."

"Dad, these brokerages are fixed? And for any type of transactions I do with him would he charge the same brokerage?"

"There are two layers of answers to your questions. See, brokerage that a broker charges may differ from client to client but generally it would be almost same. But such discretions are taken by the broker based on the volume of the transactions by a client. If you are an active client with frequent buying and selling of shares then the brokerages could be lower and if you are not active the same could be slightly higher.

"Secondly, brokerages are charged on two types of transactions - Delivery Brokerage which is for buying today and selling at a later date. Such brokerages would be charged differently; for example, 0.30% of the buying price. If you happen to buy 100 shares of ITC at Rs.350 then you would have to pay Rs.351.05 (Rs.350 x 0.30%) plus applicable levies. Once you buy this today, then you can sell the same any time in the future and again you would be charged a delivery brokerage of 0.30%. For instance, if you were to sell the same ITC 100 shares at Rs.400 after one year then your actual selling price would be Rs.398.80 (Rs.400 x 0.30%) plus applicable levies. The brokerage would get added to the price when you buy and the brokerage would get deducted from the price when you sell."

"Alright, it is pretty clear now. What about for traders, dad? Would that be any different?"

"Of course, it would be different. Usually the frequency of the trades done by traders are quite high compared to delivery based investors hence the broker gives a very competitive price to encourage traders to trade. Here we may assume the traders as Intraday Traders who typically complete their transactions during the same day. For example, a trader might buy 100 shares of Infosys at Rs.2000 today morning and irrespective of profit or a loss he would square-off his position by selling 100 shares before the market closes at 3.30 pm. This kind of a trader may do several such transactions a day which could lead to a high volume. So to provide them the right incentive to conduct such trades the brokerages could be as low as 0.02% to 0.05% of the contract value. For example, on 100 shares of Infosys buy and sell at Rs.2000 and Rs.2025 respectively the brokerage could be Rs.2000 x 0.05% (Rs.2001 actual buying price) and Rs.2025 x 0.05% (Rs.2023.99 actual selling price). In this case too apart from the brokerage charged the other levies would be added to the final buying/selling price."

"Now I got it dad. I always wondered the difference between trading and investing. It is clear now. Thank you again for sharing this invaluable information."

"You are welcome son. I hope you would make use of the learning."

-10-

INVESTING IN STOCKS & MAINTAINING A PORTFOLIO

"Dad, this is my colleague Shilpa's father's demat statement. Shilpa complains that her father has not been making adequate profits over the last many years despite having invested in many companies. Can you check this and give your advice?"

"Ok, let me see the holding statement. It is all of 5 pages....umm... quantities are in single & double digits. 5 shares, 8 shares, 10 shares, 25 shares, 50 shares. What is this? I have never heard of a few names of the companies in my life."

"Yes, dad, it seems he used to purchase stocks on news given by various people including stock brokers, friends, colleagues, media and newspapers. But having so many stocks he should have made good money, no?"

"Adi, stock holding statement is not a flower garden. A portfolio is not about quantity, it is about quality. What is the point in purchasing every stock that you see being recommended by various people? First we should plan our investments on certain parameters."

"So where was the problem, dad?"

"The problem has been in the approach. Random purchases, purchasing out of herd mentality and purchasing without defined objectives are the bane of many investors. The first step before we purchase stocks should be to define our own risk profile."

"How can we define our risk profile dad?"

"There are two types of capital that we would usually have. One is risk-free capital and the other risk capital. Basic human nature is to protect the capital by investing in assured returns such as bank or post office instruments. If we are intending to achieve returns over and above the risk-free opportunities then we have to decide how much extra return that we need and in how many days/weeks/months/years that we am willing to stay invested to achieve it."

"Can you please elaborate dad."

"We should never invest money in such opportunities that are not meant for risky opportunities such as equity market, gold/silver or other commodities on a short term basis. Only those funds with us which can be treated as risk capital should be exposed to risky assets. Once you are able to decide on the returns that you want in excess of risk-free return such as a fixed deposits (FDs), you are defining yourself clearly about your risk profile."

"If I am looking to achieve 5%-6% more than the current bank FD returns am I defining my risk dad?"

"Of course you are. If the prevailing bank FD rates are at 9% and you are looking for 5% - 6% more, you are in the range of 15% annualized returns making you a moderately aggressive investor. In fact, we can classify individuals with their returns & risk by categorizing them as

(1) Ultra Conservative - seeking assured returns, which is 9% p.a. on bank fixed deposits (March 2015)
(2) Conservative - 9% to 12% p.a. returns
(3) Moderately Conservative - 12% to 15% p.a. returns
(4) Moderately Aggressive - 15% to 18% p.a. returns
(5) Aggressive - 18% to 25% p.a. returns and
(6) Ultra Aggressive - 25% p.a. & above

All returns are on compounded annualized basis."

"Cool dad. I can now clearly identify which category I fall under. What next?"

"Once you decide on the returns you expect then you should start choosing your investments which at least clears a lot of expectations about the outcome of the chosen investment. Many people do not realize their risk taking ability, but still choose risky investments which should be avoided at all costs.

"Further, a couple of factors have to be borne in mind before beginning to purchase stocks. First is we should identify the sectors that we should be investing, second is to shortlist the stocks, third is to identify the market-capitalization of the stocks and the last is the weights of the sectors & stocks."

"Hold it dad. It is going off my head."

"Don't worry, I will make it simpler. See, generally "sectors" are what that defines the growth and as a thumb rule we can consider that if a sector does well the stocks within the sector would do well, though there may be no guarantee of that. Hence, it is ideal to start picking stocks after identifying sectors. For example, if you perceive, after studying through various research reports that IT, Banking, Capital Goods, Pharmaceutical, FMCG (fast moving consumer goods), Infrastructure, Automobiles & Power sectors are expected to do well in the long term, you should start picking stocks from these sectors."

"After that dad."

"Stocks are classified based on market capitalizations such as

Mega Cap - Rs.50000 crore & above,
Large Cap - Rs.5000 crore to Rs.5000 crore
Mid Cap - Rs.2500 crore to Rs.5000 crore
Small Cap - Rs.1000 crore to Rs.2500 crore
Micro Cap stocks - below Rs.1000 crore."

"Dad, how to know about market capitalization"

"This information is generally quoted in various research reports by the analysts and also easily available on websites of stock exchanges such as National Stock Exchange (www.nseindia.com) & Bombay Stock Exchange (www.bseindia.com) and on renowned sites such as www.moneycontrol.com. Such details can be accessed on the websites of your chosen stockbroker as well who these days provide such information for the benefit of their clients. But the easiest way to understand it is - the total number of equity shares that are issued by the company multiplied by the current market price of a stock gives us the Full Market Capitalization of a company. Further, market capitalization can be classified as Full Market Cap and Free-float Market Cap. And to arrive at the Free-float Market Capitalization only those shares that are in the hands of the public is calculated; also termed as “tradable” shares or “outstanding” shares in the market; these shares exclude shares held by promoters, group promoters, strategic stake-holders, employee holding under lock-in. Generally Free-float Market Capitalization is considered for all analysis and calculations which is said to offer clear picture of how big the company is.”

“Can you quote some examples?”

“Sure. Let me check my laptop. See, as on 5th March 2015 the Full Market Cap of Infosys was Rs.2.58 lakh crore while the Free-Float Market Cap was Rs.2.32 lakh crores making it a Mega Cap stock; Bank of Baroda’s Full Market Cap was Rs.39000 crore and the Free-Float Market Cap was Rs.17000 crore making it a Large Cap stock. Further, Biocon’s Full Market Cap was Rs.9000 crore while its Free-Float Market Cap was Rs.3000 crore making it a Mid-cap stock. Jet Airways stock had a Full Market Cap of Rs.4800 crore and a Free-Float market cap of Rs.2400 crore making it a Small Cap stock. And finally GVK Power & Infrastructure Ltd. stock’s Full Market Cap was Rs.1500 crore and its Free-Float Market Cap was Rs.680 crore making it a Micro-Cap Stock.”

“Super dad it is looking interesting.”

“And remember, the difference between Full Market Cap and Free-Float Market Cap is the portion or stake held by the promoter/group promoters that are not available for trading in the normal market. Further, like I just mentioned all these information are available and accessible on the stock exchange websites or stock brokers’ websites. We just don’t bother to check that’s all. Once you define your risk & return profile then start identifying the sectors you would like to invest with balanced weights to each of them.”

"Please explain dad."

"For instance let's say you choose the aggressive route of investing in stocks expecting returns in excess of 18% p.a. then you may have selected to invest in Automobile, Banking, Capital Goods, Financial Services, FMCG, IT and Pharmaceutical, then you perhaps can give weights of 15% to Automobile, 10% to Banking, 10% to Capital Goods, 20% to Financial Services, 10% to FMCG, 15% to IT, and 20% to Pharmaceutical. This completes your sector selection process."

"Wow it has started to look so systematic. Next we should be selecting stocks from these sectors, isn't it dad?"

"Good, you are already learning. In each of the chosen sectors you can choose a minimum of 2 and a maximum of 4 stocks which could have a mix of mega, large, mid, small & micro-cap stocks based on your risk profile. For example, if you have a conservative approach towards your returns then you could choose to have more of mega and large cap stocks and lower exposure to mid-cap stocks. Similarly, if you want to take the aggressive route then you can have lesser exposure to mega & large cap stocks by increasing the exposure to mid and small cap stocks."

"Sounds awesome way of investing in stocks dad, though the process looks very laborious."

"Money making is not easy Adi, one has to sweat to earn higher returns. No pain, no gain. While buying a shirt or a pair of socks we make so much of research and spend so much of time, but why not invest similar time before investing in stocks?"

"The logic is great dad."

"Of course it is. I shall share a model portfolio with you which would give you an idea as to how portfolios can be made and maintained."

"Super dad, thanks for your invaluable advice. I shall share this information with Shilpa and her dad. I am sure they would change their approach to investing in stocks."

"Yes you could do that. You may also share the model portfolio that I will send it to you."

"Please dad, share it with me."

-11-

MUTUAL FUND INVESTING & INVESTOR PROFILES

"Dad, I need to sit with you for some free advice."

"All advices given to you all these years have been free only son, tell me what is that you are looking for?"

"Dad, I got some good incentive this quarter and I want to start investing in mutual funds. That is what I wanted to seek your advice for."

"It seems you have transformed and my free advices have been worth after all. Tell me how much you have in mind to start investing."

"I have received about Rs.1.00 lakh as my incentives and monthly I think I can easily afford Rs.10000. I am keeping some money for my personal requirements."

"No problem son, it is not good to invest all the money that you earn, you should spend too, and this is the age for you to spend and enjoy life. But be careful not to splurge on unnecessary things."

"Thanks dad, I thought you would scold me."

"I believe that there is no point in living frugally when you are young and save for an old age when you may not enjoy what you have saved. At the same time you have to make wise decisions about how much to set aside for investing after provisioning for spending."

"True dad, now tell me how to plan my investments in mutual funds."

"I suggest you start investing in mutual funds rather than resorting to buying stocks directly from the stock market. Keep your exposure to stocks limited and increase exposure to mutual funds. Since you are just beginning your investing journey mutual funds would be ideal to build long term wealth and also it offers better stock diversification."

"Yes, a few of my colleagues too are investing in mutual funds."

"Okay then if you do not need the funds at least for the next 5 years you should consider investing in equity mutual funds."

"I think I will not need it immediately. I am confident of getting good incentives this quarter too and I shall plan that money for something else."

"First let's understand what mutual funds are. Mutual funds are collective investment schemes that mobilizes monies from investors who seek to attain returns those are better than a bank deposit and also offers them some diversification across asset classes. Through a three tier structure a mutual fund house is created. There will be a sponsor company, a board of trustees and asset management company. Since the funds of investors are managed by an unknown entity to create a strong trust or belief in the management of funds and securities a Trust is created to ensure the transactions take place with a lot of rules, regulations and procedures."

"Dad, does SEBI takes care of mutual funds?"

"Yes, very much. Securities Exchange Board of India is the market regulator for mutual funds too and the mutual fund house has to adhere to the rules and regulations as prescribed by them and the motto of SEBI is to protect investors' interest and they are doing a great job of regulating it."

"How does the concept of mutual fund work dad? I have always been curious about their method of operations?"

"In fact, Adi, it is very fascinating to understand how fabulously this system of fund management works. See, generally everyone wants to earn higher returns and they are not happy with the returns that a fixed deposit generates because these types of fixed income products are neither designed to overcome inflation nor create wealth. They just generate a regular income by way of interest. To meet the growing need of people who seek inflation beating returns a formal and organized financial markets were created by way of debt and equity markets. Mutual funds actively participate as a financial intermediary by seeking opportunities to invest and generate returns that can beat or outperform the bank deposit or post office savings returns. For those who seek safety or low risk, mutual fund houses accessed debt market such as money market and bond market where the surplus monies of interested people gets deployed and returns generated by way of interest income which gets distributed. For those who sought higher returns over safety the monies were invested in equity markets. To sum up, to generate income debt markets became an ideal destination wherein a common investor could not have directly accessed and he could access through debt mutual funds. Similarly, for capital appreciation or growth instead of investing directly in stock markets a common investor or a lay investor entrusted his investable money to a fund house to invest on his or her behalf."

"Is it safe to invest through mutual funds?"

"I am not sure what you mean by safe here. But let me explain. Mutual funds are not safe as an investment because they are accessing both debt and equity markets which has different types of risks associated with them. While the risks in debt markets are low it does not mean it is risk-free. A fund manager is believed to have the ability to manage such risks through his/her professional capabilities of understanding and managing risk. Though the risk is low, capital depreciation in all cases cannot be ruled out.

"When it comes to equity, the risk is high to very high. Since stock markets are risky by nature by way of different types of risks associated the possibility of capital erosion cannot be ruled out. With debt the capital may depreciate but with equity the capital may be fully eroded. But a fund manager would be in a position to manage such risks through his management capabilities. It is a very niche and professional job which fund houses manage by engaging some brilliant fund managers. A terrible market condition can challenge the ability of a fund manager. Hence, it would be prudent to carefully choose the fund house and the fund manager before investing."

"Cool dad. It sounds pretty professional."

"Yes mutual funds are a terrific concept. Thanks to the government that introduced this concept in India way back in 1963-64 by way of Unit Trust of India or UTI. The total assets managed across debt and equity as in March 2015 had been Rs.12 lakh crore which is a pretty good number. Over the last few years it has grown really big with a potential to grow bigger. New participants and young investors like you would surely add to the numbers."

"Surely I will invest in mutual funds dad. I now feel instead of buying stocks directly I would opt for investing through mutual funds. There is no headache. I will pay for the expenses to a fund house and they will take care of research and investment management."

"That's great. Mutual funds are designed to meet the requirement of different types of investor profiles."

"Dad how will I know what type of an investor I am? I mean my profile."

"I already explained this to you last time around that investors can be classified from being Ultra Conservative to Ultra Aggressive based on their expected returns from any investments. You have forgotten about that?"

"Oh no dad, I clearly remember. It is those who expect lower returns to those who expect higher returns; from 9% to about 25% returns. Am I right?"

"Yes. Unless such classifications are not being done it would be difficult to gauge the risk taking ability. But at your age you should adopt aggressive investing strategy which should be tempered down as you age. You should put yourselves in the category of expecting returns in the range of 15% to 18% compounded over the future years."

"Now it sounds simple, dad."

"Yes, actually it is. In mutual funds there are objective driven schemes that can suit every type of risk & return profile investors. In fact, mutual funds are called as ***funds for all seasons & all reasons***."

"Sounds interesting; then which scheme should I choose?"

"Don't rush it Adi. There are more than 40 mutual fund companies who have rolled out over 500 equity schemes and it can get complicated to choose your choice of schemes."

"Wow, I didn't know that."

"Before you begin investing in equity oriented schemes first you have to choose the theme such as

- Balanced Funds (indicatively 65% equity; 35% debt)
- Index Funds (investing only in either Sensex or Nifty stocks; passive fund management)
- Large Cap oriented (investing largely in large cap stocks)
- Large & Mid-cap oriented (higher exposure to large & mid cap stocks)
- Multi-cap oriented (investing across all types of market caps in different proportions)
- Mid-cap oriented (investing largely in mid-cap stocks)
- Mid & Small-cap oriented (higher exposure to mid & small cap stocks)
- Small-cap oriented (investing largely in small-cap stocks)
- Micro-cap oriented (investing largely in micro-cap stocks)
- Dynamic (can move 100% from equity to debt and debt to equity based on market conditions)
- Contra (going against the market trend; buy when market is selling & vice versa)
- Thematic (investing in themes such as infra, consumption, financial services)
- Sector (specific sectors such as auto, FMCG, Pharma, IT, Banking etc.)
- Fund of Funds (investing in different mutual fund schemes managed by different fund houses)
- Global themes (investing in international stocks)

The above classification is to meet the risk and return expectation of different types of investors. All these are equity oriented schemes except for Balanced Funds which is called as Equity Hybrid since it has exposure to debt to the extent of 35%. Within the accepted risk category index funds and balanced funds are considered to be at the bottom of the risk table while thematic & sector funds are at the top."

"Oh, dad, so many themes, how should I choose?"

"Yes, these many themes are designed to meet the risk & returns profile of different type of investors as I mentioned earlier with the typical investor profiles. So in your case we will start with lump sum investing and then address the systematic investing."

"Right dad I am all ears."

"Since you said you are not in need of this amount for at least 5 years I suggest a portfolio comprising of 25% in Large Cap themes; 15% in Large & Mid-cap themes, 15% in Multi-cap themes, 25% in Mid Cap themes and balance 20% in Small & Mid-cap themes. Maximum five themes are okay for you to invest."

"Sounds very systematic way of investing, but will I achieve my expected returns?"

"Listen, it is not possible to predict the market performance, at the same time you should trust the stock market because in the past it has proven to be a true wealth creator comparable to other asset classes. We have to invest based on certain assumptions such as how much the market can perform on an annual basis over the future years. Here I mean market means Index. Assuming even if the broad-based index such as Sensex or Nifty offers returns of 12% to 15% on CAGR (compounded annual growth rate) basis, by diversifying into different types of themes such as Large caps, Mid-caps, Multi-cap and Mid & Small-cap funds there are enough reasons to believe that you should be able to achieve 15% and more over the next 5 years. If you calculate the returns of BSE's broad based index Sensex from Dec 2009 till Dec 2014 the compounded returns had been 10.50% while Birla SL Frontline Equity Fund, a large-cap oriented equity scheme, gave compounded annual return of 15%

in the same duration of 5 years (CRISIL Rating 4 stars; courtesy www.moneycontrol.com). Similarly, ICICI Pru Value Discovery Fund, a mid & small cap oriented equity scheme offered a compounded annual return of 22% during the same Dec 2009 to Dec 2014 tenure (CRISIL Rating 3 stars; courtesy www.moneycontrol.com). Respective fund managers thrive to beat the market performance while they are managing their portfolios."

"Wow that is a super duper performance from the fund houses. But why have you not suggested to invest in balanced & index funds?"

"For your type of risk & return profile having Balanced & Index Funds would be too defensive and you may not be able to achieve your desired CAGR (compounded annual gross return); with that assumption I have not considered these two themes. Also I have ignored Thematic & Sector focussed themes because they are very aggressive and at this juncture you should best avoid them. You can use them as "discretionary", meaning if it is very necessary."

"Right dad. I got it now."

"I have suggested to have large cap oriented themes in your portfolio which is very essential for every type of investor portfolios because large caps act as cushion across market performances. It is like having Sachin Tendulkar, Rahul Dravid and VVS Lakshman in your cricket team who would offer a solid support in difficult situations."

"Yes, yes dad. You are absolutely right. But dad, how to decide which scheme is good to invest?"

"First you get ready with your funds I shall get you the updated details of the final investment procedures by tomorrow evening. Also you have to be registered under the KYC before beginning your mutual fund investing."

"Sure dad, I am hungry let's have lunch."

-12-

THE FUNDAMENTALS OF KYC

"Dad, I am ready to start my investments in mutual funds as suggested by you last week. Can I meet your advisor friend Prasad uncle over the weekend?"

"Yes, sure Adi, I will ask Prasad Achaiah to come over. But as per the pre-investing procedure you have to get yourself registered under the KYC norms, unless this is not done no mutual fund company will process your application."

"Dad, what is this KYC? Is it a laborious process? I don't like all these filling forms and signing in umpteen number of places."

"Hey son, hold on. There is nothing to get irritated. It is simple yet an important procedure that has been introduced by the market regulator to keep track of the source of income that an investor brings into an investment."

"Can you please be more specific dad?"

"KYC means Know Your Customer; meaning formally and officially identifying the customer identity and status. All that is needed is your passport size colour photograph, self-attested copies of your PAN card and any one of these address proofs such as voter's ID, driving license, passport, bank passbook, aadhaar card or BSNL/MTNL telephone bill to be submitted along with a one page application form duly filled with personal information, bank account details and signed. Fill it, submit it and start investing."

"Is that so simple?"

"Of course it is that simple. Once you submit it to any of the mutual fund companies they will process the KYC application and upload the status by offering you a status termed as "KYC Verified". You don't have to repeat this process again and again during any of your future mutual fund investments. This is a one-time procedure. All mutual fund companies can access your information through the help of your PAN number and accept your future investments either in debt or equity schemes without any hassles."

"Dad why has this been introduced? I think they should have made it simpler by just asking people to invest picking up a mutual fund application form."

"Even now the process is quite simple. Listen Adi, most of the source of income in India is still not accounted officially and there is a strain on tax collection with unaccounted funds coming into the organized sector. By this KYC process the market regulator is streamlining the process of money flow by identifying the persons/entities investing in financial instruments and their source of income."

"Oh, now I am able to understand why producing PAN card has been mandatory for almost all financial transactions."

"Absolutely; if a country's economy has to flourish people will have to declare their income and source of such income and pay taxes. This will help the country to be self-sustained in terms of finances and the governments do not have to borrow money from external sources and pay hefty interests on such borrowings to run the country. The picture is much larger than you can imagine."

"I did not think from this angle at all, dad."

"We have to be responsible citizens first. Further, there is a strong Anti-Money Laundering Act that is enacted to curb any illegal money that might enter the financial markets which is a heinous crime. To ensure that such monies are not part of any investments done by investors by obtaining certain basic documents a KYC Verified status has been put in place."

"Yes dad understood, please get my KYC done."

"Sure I will. Remember son, all these procedures are to ensure that we are earning our income that is accounted for and the profit we may get from such investments are accounted too. If all the citizens are accounting their source of income and paying taxes the obvious effect is that the economy flourishes which in fact is good for the people."

-13-

MUTUAL FUNDS - OPTIONS TO INVEST LUMP SUM & SYSTEMATIC / DIRECT & REGULAR PLAN / GROWTH & DIVIDEND

"Dad, Prasad uncle has left these application forms to be filled, could you please sit with me while I fill these?"

"You are already 25 years and you should know how to fill these forms son. I only had told Prasad to leave it and you would complete filling these forms."

"But if you are with me I get to learn a few new aspects dad, I am a bit selfish you see!"

"Okay, you cunning fellow get me those forms and let's start filling it."

"Dad, Prasad uncle was saying I should invest as lump sum and systematic so he has given two different types of forms. Could you please help me with this?"

"Yes. To invest one time amount is termed as "lump sum" investing and to invest a fixed amount each month is termed as "systematic". Since you had said you have about a lakh rupee with you, you can first choose to invest through the lump sum route. I will give you a portfolio format which would have the segregation of the themes and schemes with weights to each of the themes and schemes based on that you fill the forms."

"Alright dad. I will do that way. Also I wanted to know if I have to mention how long I will stay invested in the chosen schemes."

"No, that information is not asked by the mutual fund company at all. The duration of investing is as per your financial planning. If you invest in a debt fund where the fund is investing in fixed income securities you would usually be doing for a duration of about 3 years and if you have longer duration with wealth creation in mind, usually about 5 years and above, then you would choose equity oriented mutual fund themes and schemes.

"Further, you are allowed to withdraw or redeem your investments as per your choice of a date of the future. For example, you have an event coming in the next few weeks or months you would have obviously chosen a short term debt scheme and you would withdraw when the date of such event comes closer. Similarly, if you have some events happening after 5 years you would choose to withdraw when such events start happening at a future date. Basically mutual fund investments are event based and as decided or required by the investor. The mutual fund company does not involve in your investing decisions. They only accept your investment, invest in various opportunities of debt and/or equity, manage to the best of their abilities and return your money at the prevailing unit values (prevailing NAVs) whenever you ask for it. If the NAV has gone up you would have made a gain, if it would have fallen you would have made a loss."

"Yes, yes dad you have already explained to me about the fund management earlier. Can I withdraw when I see a profit or even a loss?"

"Of course you can. Let me explain it with an example. For example, an event is happening five years from today and you invest Rs.50000 today to meet that event. You had expected that this investment would have grown to Rs.1.00 lakh at 15% annual compounded returns in these 5 years. But at the end of 36 months you see that because of a good market performance your Rs.50000 has already grown and become Rs.1.00 lakh, at this juncture it would be a prudent decision to either withdraw the investment or shift the entire money into a debt fund and wait for the planned event to occur. This is purest method of planning your investment."

"Sounds very professional dad. But why should I withdraw if the market is doing well? I would continue to hold and try to achieve higher returns. I think I should look to maximize my returns."

"That would be quite foolish son. Always remember the moral stories that you listened to from your grandmother. "A bird in the hand is always better than two in the bush." Market is not your father's property; the performance would be based on various parameters and if you have been able to achieve such returns in such short time you would have done a wise decision to book the profit. When it comes to money greed is not good at all. Don't withdraw and keep it in your bank's savings account. You should move the money within the same fund house to a low risk debt fund such as a liquid fund or a short term debt fund and leave it to generate debt market based returns for the next 2 years and take it back when your event actually is nearing. That is what real investment literacy is."

"Got it dad. I got carried away."

"Yeah, if you become one among those who get carried away you could be swept away. Be happy when equity market performs exceedingly well and enjoy the benefits of infinite returns and power of compounding."

"Now dad, what about losses? If there is a loss to my capital while I am waiting for my investment to grow should I wait or should I exit?"

"This is a good question you have asked in a long time! Like I have told you in the past, performance of the market is uncertain. Even the performance of a fund manager can be tested due to demanding and challenging market conditions. As an investor you should keep an eye on the market performance as also the funds' performances that you have invested in. If you find that the performance of your particular scheme has fallen and market also has fallen then you need not worry, all you will have to do is wait for the markets to recover. On the contrary, if the market has been doing well but your fund is not doing well then there is something wrong with the fund management. So make your judgement or ask your advisor and exit booking losses in case it is under any losses, and move into a better performing theme and a scheme."

"Sounds good. How much should I invest as minimum amount as lump sum in a mutual fund scheme?"

"For all lump sum investments in debt or equity schemes the minimum has been pegged at Rs.5000, so you can start investing in mutual funds with as small as Rs.5000. But for some debt funds the minimum lump sum investment could be Rs.10000, you will have to check while investing."

"Okay dad, I will invest as per the portfolio recommendation. Now, what is this Growth, Dividend Pay-out and Dividend Reinvestment Option that the form is asking me to tick? Which one should I choose dad?"

"Oh yes, you need to understand this very importantly. Growth Option is provided for those who choose to stay invested without liking to withdraw intermittently. Which means today if you invest Rs.5000 at Rs.10 Net Asset Value or NAV in an equity mutual fund then you would have been allotted 500 units (Rs.5000 divided by Rs.10) by the fund house. After staying invested for a period of 15 months assuming the NAV would have grown to become Rs.12, the Rs.2 over and above Rs.10 is the growth of the investment which further means that your investment of Rs.5000 would have become Rs.6000 at 20% growth in absolute terms (500 units multiplied by Rs.12). The Rs.1000 profit would be your capital gain under the Growth Option (remember this growth would be tax-free since gains from equity after staying invested for a period of above 12 months is exempt from all types of taxes). At this juncture (after staying invested for 15 months) you could decide to continue to stay invested without withdrawing to meet your planned future objective and returns expectation. If the market does well in the future your value of investment would have grown further. Rs.12 NAV could become Rs.15, Rs.20 and more in line with the market performance. That is why it is called as a Growth Option.

"The Dividend Option has two sub options - Pay-out and Reinvestment. Under the Pay-out Option as and when the fund house decides to share the profit or the growth portion with its unitholders you would receive a dividend amount from them. For example, you invested Rs.5000 today at Rs.10 NAV in an equity mutual fund and you were allotted 500 units and you had chosen Dividend Pay-out Option; assuming 15 months from today the NAV grows to Rs.12 and the fund house decides to share the profit of Rs.2 with you; so now you would receive an amount of Rs.1000 from them as your share of the profit. You had 500 units and at Rs.2 per unit you were paid Rs.1000 (500 units x Rs.2); this amount you receive in your bank account as credit and you are free to utilize this money as per your wish, no questions asked; moreover, this entire dividend amount you received would be tax-free. After the dividend has been paid out to you the NAV would come down to Rs.10 from Rs.12 because you have en-cashed the growth portion and you will have to wait for further such dividend declaration announcements from the fund house which would be done based on the decision taken by them from time to time. Remember, dividend pay-outs are not mandatory by fund houses, they would decide to pay based on certain parameters and declaring dividends are the prerogative of the fund houses."

"Wow dad, so much to learn from a simple option!"

"Yes, without reasons these have not been introduced. Now let's understand the meaning of Dividend Reinvestment Option. This option is similar to Growth Option but the difference being the dividend pay-out amount would be reinvested into the investment and you would be having more number of units over a period of time with each dividend declaration. Let's continue with the same example of Rs.5000 invested in an equity mutual fund scheme at Rs.10 NAV and you would have received 500 units. 15 months from today when the NAV is Rs.12 the fund declares a dividend of Rs.2 per unit and you stand to receive Rs.1000, but since you had opted for reinvestment you would not receive any cash or credit of amount, instead the Rs.1000 would get converted into units. You would receive 100 units that would be credited to your earlier units of 500 taking the total units in your account to 600 units. If you multiply 600 units with Rs.10, the post dividend NAV, the valuation on that day would be Rs.6000."

"Super dad, but I didn't understand how I got that 100 units extra. Could you please explain?"

"Oh sorry, I forgot. See, the dividend declared was Rs.1000 which is part of the growth or Rs.2 per unit multiplied by 500 units; since you did not wanted to take cash by opting for reinvestment the fund house converted Rs.1000 by dividing it by the post-dividend NAV which is Rs.10 (Rs.1000 / Rs.10) and would offer you 100 additional units taking your tally of units from 500 to 600. Like this over the future as long as you stay invested in the fund without withdrawing, as and when dividends are declared the amount would get converted into units and credited to your earlier units held taking the number of units higher and higher. In the future if you need some funds to withdraw you can withdraw the units based on your need and leave the rest of the units in the fund."

"Oh I see. It is now clear how these options are different from each other. But dad, which one should I choose, growth or dividend?"

"I would recommend you choose Growth Option because, if you choose dividend pay-out option and when you receive the dividend if you spend without reinvesting it in some productive purpose then it would be a big waste. At your age it would be ideal to opt for growth option which at least makes you to stay invested for longer period of time while your investment grows without any withdrawals. Also dividend pay-out options would be good for retired people or for those who depend on tax-free dividend income to make a living. Pension income, Rental income, interest income and dividend income are some of the regular flow of income that retired people look for, so they perhaps could choose such options. But you are young and can stay invested without needing any intermittent cash-flows, so choose growth option. And also remember, reinvestment option in equity schemes are not worth it, it is similar to growth option, so don't confuse yourself by opting for this option. So growth option it is."

"Lastly dad, it is mentioned here on the application form Direct Plan, Regular Plan, Retail Plan etc. what are these?"

"Oh these plans, I will tell you. Till August 2009 investors investing in equity mutual funds were charged an Entry Load of 2.25% on the prevailing NAV and they had to mandatorily go through an advisor to invest wherein the said 2.25% was the commission or the fee these advisors used to earn on the investment amount. Since SEBI felt that many advisors were misusing this facility it decided to ban all types of entry loads from 1.8.2009. Ever since, investors are allowed to invest directly by surpassing an advisor by opting for Direct Plans which would have a lesser expense ratio (a charge that is charged by the fund to manage the scheme related expenses).

"Regular or Retail Plans are those where the investment has been routed through an advisor and even though there would be no upfront entry load the advisor would still be paid some fee by the fund house directly which is adjusted from the NAV. So basically the difference between Direct and Regular or Retail Plan is investing without the assistance of an advisor and with the assistance of an advisor. And there is another plan called as Institutional Plan which is exclusively designed for institutions or corporates who invest large amounts wherein the expense ratios for such investments would be lower. So, you can choose Regular Plan since you will be investing through Prasad Achaiah, our advisor."

"Alright dad, I will go with your advice. I shall also speak to Prasad uncle while handing over the application forms. I am sure he would have given me the same advice."

"Yes, he would have done the same. And about systematic investment plan I shall let you know about it tomorrow. I have to take your mom out for some shopping. In the meantime, I will mail you the portfolio format for lump sum investment, you fill all the application forms and remember to tick the growth option."

"Okay dad, you carry on."

-14-

SIGNIFICANCE OF SYSTEMATIC INVESTMENT PLAN or SIP

"Adi, come here. Let's see how you have filled the mutual fund application forms."

"Dad, here they are. Prasad uncle and I discussed at length about the investment plan and he was impressed with your portfolio recommendation. But dad, Prasad uncle was insisting that I should focus more on Systematic Investment Plan or SIP. I am wondering what is so special about this SIP. I also remember that you too had been investing in some SIPs earlier."

"Adi, you really do not know the power of small amounts and I have been a big beneficiary of such investments in my life. Just like my grandmother and my mother were dropping some notes and coins in a piggy bank to meet their future events in the absence of a formal financial opportunity, systematic investment plan is similar to that concept done in an organized manner. Even a bank or post office recurring deposit can be an example for systematic investment plan but in a debt or fixed income product."

"Yes dad, I know. Many people invest in recurring deposits where they pay a fixed amount each month for a fixed period of time at some fixed rate of interest."

"You are absolutely right. Though recurring deposits or RDs are a good method to invest for a future event, they are unfortunately not designed to create wealth or even beat inflation. The idea here is to protect the capital than to build wealth since the returns are very nominal and may not suffice over longer period of time to meet various life events. RD should be one of the systematic investments one should choose, not the only one."

"How the mutual fund SIP is different from RD dad?"

"Let me explain in detail: Systematic investment plan that you are being recommended by Prasad is to invest a predetermined fixed amount each month in an equity mutual fund that invests in equity stocks by a professional asset management company managed by professional fund managers. It provides indirect access to stock market which reduces the pain or the process of researching and investing which can eat into our productive time.

"If lump sum investment is to invest money one time, Systematic Investment Plan (SIP) is to invest a predetermined amount over a predetermined period of time. For example, if you were to spare Rs.1000 each month for a period of 5 years to meet a foreseen event you could choose the SIP route of investing in a specific equity mutual fund. Similarly you can predetermine your future event or events and then suitably choose the number of years you may want to stay invested.

"Importantly you have to understand about SIP in equity oriented schemes is that it offers the benefit what is termed as "rupee-cost averaging" which means your monthly investment would purchase units based on the prevailing net asset values (NAVs) and each month the units allotted would vary due to changes in the market performance that invariably leads to change in the NAVs.

"To explain with an example, if you have decided to invest Rs.1000 on 10th of each month starting from April 2014 in an equity oriented mutual fund scheme, on the first month (assuming 10.04.2014 the NAV was Rs.10) you would have been allotted 100 units (Rs.1000 divided by Rs.10); next month on 10.05.2014 assuming the NAV had risen to Rs.10.20 then you would be allotted 98.039 units; on the third month on 10.06.2014 if the NAV had fallen to Rs.9.75 you would be allotted Rs.102.56. You can notice that at different NAV levels different units get allotted (lower units when the NAV rises and higher units when the NAV reduces) and over the chosen period of your monthly investment you would have been allotted a chunk of units in line with the market performance and the NAVs thereon leading you to have accumulated such units which when withdrawn or redeemed at the end of the period or a date as decided by you could have gained significantly; this method of accumulating units is what I mentioned to you as "rupee-cost averaging". I shall share a real-time example of such possibility with you which would give you a clear understanding of the concept."

"Awesome dad. The possibility looks infinite considering that the markets are volatile and we can accumulate units at different levels of the market performances."

"Absolutely. There is no need to time the market, just keep investing ignoring the daily market fluctuations and concentrate on accumulating units and then see the magic of "power of compounding" and "magic of equities".

"Surely it sounds worth exploring dad."

"Yes it is, thousands of people have benefited from such a systematic practice and there is nothing to doubt why you too should not benefit. Now, you were saying you could spare Rs.10000 per month regularly; this amount can be split into, perhaps, five SIPs by investing Rs.2000 in five different types of themes and schemes which would help you meeting various future life events across various time period."

"How to choose how many years should I invest in SIP dad? Should I specify such information in the application form before investing?"

"Good question Adi. You have to remember that all investments are done for specific purposes of life which can be termed as "foreseen events". For investing in SIP choosing a minimum period of 5 years is recommended because such kind of time would be required to get inflation beating returns from equity markets. For instance, you are almost 25 years now and assuming you will want to invest in a house five years from today for which you would like to avail a bank loan; if the cost of the property would be Rs.50 lakhs, then an amount of Rs.10 lakh would be your part of investment before the bank sanctions you a loan of Rs.40 lakhs. So, how would you create this Rs.10 lakhs?

Such an amount can be created if you start SIPs from this month itself. To create a corpus of Rs.10 lakhs at 12% annual compounded returns you will have to invest about Rs.12000 each month for 60 months. When you are filling the application form of a mutual fund scheme you can choose dates by way of month and year based on such future event or events and invest. If you are starting to invest this month that is April 2015 then you will mention that you would invest Rs.12000 each month in about 4 different schemes and themes of Rs.3000 each till March 2020 of four different fund houses. Depending on the performance of the market and the schemes and themes you have chosen you could reach your desired expectation of achieving Rs.10 lakhs."

"Okay, but why in different schemes and themes and fund houses? Why not invest the entire Rs.12000 in one scheme, one theme and one fund house. It would be much easier isn't it dad?"

"Good doubt you have raised son. See, a fund manager is not God. He too is a human being. Generally all fund managers try and perform to the best of their abilities, but sometimes they too can go wrong with wrong calls, wrong outcome of a research conducted before investing in specific securities and similar such problems and constraints. Hence, to avoid such situations it would be better if you do not have a concentrated exposure of all your investments in one fund house; it would be better if your investments are spread across different fund houses and also try and get the flavour of different fund managers capability of fund management skills."

"Understood dad. Anything else that I should keep in mind?"

"Another aspect which I have already discussed with you, but will say it again is that you should maintain a portfolio based investment pattern for SIPs too. You should split the investments into different themes. For example, an amount of Rs.12000 can be invested in this split fashion: Rs.3000 each in a Large Cap oriented, Multi-cap oriented, Mid Cap oriented and Balance Fund. This, perhaps, would give you the right diversification for the kind of returns you are expecting. And for these four themes you can choose four different mutual fund companies based on research which Prasad would help you with.

Further, first you should list out all your future requirements that needs money, something like we had discussed once before called as Financial Planning. Now you are single or unmarried hence your needs would be less or limited, but once you are married your needs would change and when you have children the needs would further change including your priorities. So life is full of events with different life goals at different stages of your life. But you should keep planning for all such events and being systematic is what would help you to meet such events and equity SIPs offer such accessibility and simplicity to meet such events."

"What about risks of investing in SIPs dad? Are there any?"

"There are risks son, when we are seeking higher returns risks are common. Since equity markets are exposed to several types of risks the capital protection is not guaranteed. But going by the last 20 years of good mutual fund schemes' performances I would without any reservations say that most schemes have weathered the market uncertainties very well. I will share such real-time data with you and I am sure you would be surprised with the final outcome. The ability of the fund managers are tested by difficult and challenging markets and that is the reason you would need the assistance of an advisor who would guide you with good themes and schemes. Also each fund house would adopt certain risk mitigation strategies to address such challenges and we have to believe in their abilities. There are several illustrious fund managers from equally illustrious fund houses who have done really well with their fund management over the years. And remember, long duration of investing ideas usually have worked in favour of the investor. So don't worry, you are still young and you can bear some risks on your way to reaching your financial objectives."

"Sure dad. Will call Prasad uncle and finalize my SIP investments."

"Yeah do that. I will share some data with you by email."

-15-

ABOUT EQUITY LINKED SAVINGS SCHEME OR ELSS AS A TAX SAVING INSTRUMENT

"Sorry dad, I keep pestering you a lot about investment knowledge. One more information I need from you. My company is asking me if they can deduct some money from my salary towards Income Tax that I may have to pay by next March. I wanted to check with you how to save on taxes."

"Don't worry son, knowledge should not be kept to oneself; it has to be imparted. I don't want to die as a knowledgeable person, but a person who also imparted it. I am glad that you keep asking me some interesting queries on investments. Whatever I know I keep sharing with you with all earnest."

"I know dad, I can take that liberty from you."

"The great Albert Einstein said, "The hardest thing to understand in the world is the income tax." See, it is a human trait that we do not want to part with our money, and taxes are something which we all hate to pay. We need to be threatened or we need to be incentivized, only then we act. Fortunately, government chose the latter option of incentivising the tax payers by way of various Sections under the Income Tax Act, 1961.

"The biggest opportunity is created under the IT Act is Section 80C wherein one can invest up to Rs.1.50 lakhs (as on financial year 2014-15) in various earmarked tax saving instruments and claim tax exemptions. There are several investment opportunities provided ranging from dedicated locked-in fixed deposits to post office savings to insurance premiums to home loan principal component to tuition fees to provident fund contribution and importantly investing in Equity Linked Saving Scheme or ELSS. I am going to tell you more about this opportunity since the rest are self-explanatory and mostly designed to protect the capital.

"To refrain people (tax savers) from concentrating their tax saving investments only in debt oriented products & insurances, to promote equity investments at the grass-root level government introduced ELSS as another opportunity to save taxes. The mutual fund houses (asset management companies) were allowed to design and structure exclusive equity portfolios that should be compulsorily locked-in for a period of 3 years and investments done in these schemes were exempted from paying taxes with a maximum investment limit of Rs.1.50 lakhs."

"Dad, you are telling investments in ELSS would be locked-in for 3 years?"

"Yes, you would not be allowed to withdraw for three years from the date of such investments. One significant advantage of this opportunity is that it allows you to stay invested for a period of three years which is some sort of a long term investment plan considering that equity markets are volatile and the purpose of equities are to offer capital gains over longer period of time."

"But dad, is it worth investing in equity linked tax saving schemes? Aren't they risky?"

"Again you are back with your "equities are risky" slogan. Chill son. You are not being asked to invest all your money in equity oriented opportunity, even if you consider investing 20% of Rs.1.50 lakhs which would be Rs.30000, it would be enough. Rest you go ahead and invest in other opportunities. Don't tell me you can't afford even such a small risk."

"Sorry dad, I know you get angry when anyone says equities are risky. I will not say that again. Now tell me how should I go about investing? Any particular method of investing that I need to follow?"

"Equities no doubt are risky, but you should learn how to convert that riskiness into opportunity, there lies the acumen. If you check some of the best performing ELSS schemes' performances over the last 3 to 5 years you would not be saying this. Check out these performances:

Axis Long Term Equity Fund - Growth Plan (3 years CAGR 36.60%; 5 years CAGR 23.90%)
ICICI Pru Tax Plan - Growth Plan (3 years CAGR 26.70%; 5 years CAGR 16.80%)
Reliance Tax Saver - Growth Plan (3 years CAGR 32.90%; 5 years CAGR 21.50%)
Birla SL Tax Relief 96 - Growth Plan (3 years CAGR 29.90%; 5 years CAGR 15.50%)
Franklin India Tax Shield - Growth Plan (3 years CAGR 26.90%; 5 years CAGR 18.30%)

(Source: www.moneycontrol.com as on 17.03.2015)

"So the moral of the story is some risks are worth exploring. Besides the tax saving opportunity ELSS can also offer inflation beating returns which is the purpose these are designed and the gains at the end of 3 years is fully exempt from any taxes since it qualifies for long term capital gains which is exempt for equity investments if withdrawn after a year of staying invested."

"Yes, I remember that dad. Now, which route to choose? Lump sum or SIP?"

"Both these options depend on the investor's choice. Usually most tax saving decisions are made towards the year end where individuals would be choosing lump sum since the time left to invest would be very less. For those who may not be able to afford lump sum, systematic route by way of SIPs would be ideal. For example, from the month of April this year if you choose ELSS to invest a total of Rs.30000 out of the given Rs.1.50 lakhs under Sec 80C you can invest Rs.2500 each month which could help you to reach the desired amount (Rs.2500 x 12 months) before the financial year ends in March. This would be the easiest method to avoid last minute running around to arrange large amounts of money. It is all about planning that's all."

"Okay dad, understood. Anything else I should bear in mind about ELSS investments?"

"Yes there are a couple of more aspects that you should bear in mind. First, if you are choosing SIP route of investing in ELSS you would not be allowed to withdraw / redeem unless each of the month's investment does not complete 36 months from the date of such investments, because each investment would be treated as fresh investment each month and you would be allowed to withdraw or redeem only after completion of 36 months from the dates of such investments. For example, if you have chosen 36 months of SIP in an ELSS scheme, then your 36th month investment (the last investment) would be allowed to withdraw after 36 months from that month. I hope you got what I am saying?"

"Yes dad, I think I understood. You mean to say that since the lock-in period of ELSS is 36 months my each month investment would be allowed to withdraw upon completion of 36 months from date of such investment. For instance, my 18th month investment of Rs.2500 would be allowed to be redeemed 36 months from that month. Am I right?"

"Absolutely right, you would have to stay invested for a longer period to redeem all your investments done in those 36 months. So, before investing you should know this fact. I will write and show you some examples as to how it works. See here:

ILLUSTRATION:

Date of Invt.	SIP Amount	Withdrawal date
01.04.2015	Rs.2500	01.04.2018
01.05.2015	Rs.2500	01.05.2018
01.09.2016	Rs.2500	01.09.2019
01.10.2016	Rs.2500	01.10.2019
01.07.2017	Rs.2500	01.07.2020
01.08.2017	Rs.2500	01.08.2020
01.02.2018	Rs.2500	01.02.2021
01.03.2018	Rs.2500	01.03.2021

"Secondly, you can choose Growth, Dividend Pay-out or Dividend Reinvestment Option. If you choose Growth Option then any profit would remain in your investment and if the scheme is performing well then your investment value too would continue to grow as long as you stay invested. After the completion of the mandatory staying period of three years you can decide to redeem your units in full or partial as per your wish.

"In the next Dividend Pay-out Option profits would be paid out in the form of dividends which you are free to receive and enjoy. Since the dividends are tax free you can indeed enjoy that pay-out or even plan to reinvest that in some other investment opportunity. But you have to note that once the dividend is paid out the NAV of the scheme would have reduced. I have already shared the process earlier with you of how dividend pay-out and reinvestment calculations work.

"Another option is Dividend Reinvestment wherein additional units would get added to your original units after the dividend pay-out amount gets converted into units. In fact, you can use these dividend reinvestment units as fresh purchase during the year if dividends get declared and credited and show as fresh investment in ELSS for that specific financial year which can be pretty advantageous. And such reinvested units again are not allowed to be redeemed for 36 months from the date of such credits.

"For example, during 2015-16 had you invested Rs.50000 in an ELSS scheme where you had chosen Dividend Reinvestment Option and if the fund declares a dividend wherein you were allotted 500 additional units, these new units and the value thereon can be treated as a fresh investment for the year over and above the Rs.50000 that you had invested. Understood?"

"But dad, I think this reinvestment option in ELSS scheme is something like a whirlpool, we cannot get out easily even after we stop investing in that scheme. Is my understanding right?"

"Atta boy, you have become smarter than I had imagined! You are bang-on right with your understanding. This reinvestment option should be best avoided; that would indeed be a whirlpool since as long as the fund house continues to give dividends I keep getting new units allotted which again gets under lock-in for three years and the saga continues. I wonder why this option is still available under ELSS."

"Yes dad, sounds pretty confusing. So, should I choose growth or dividend pay-out option?"

"I think you should stick to growth option since I am not sure if you would be reinvesting the dividends that you would receive in better options and moreover such dividend pay-outs are not guaranteed; it all depends on the market and fund's performance. Maybe those who seek some tax-free income should opt for pay-out options."

"Great dad. I shall decide in a day or two if I would choose the SIP route or the lump sum route. I shall speak to Prasad uncle as well. Thanks dad, for such detailed explanation. I can share this information with my colleagues as well."

"Yeah sure, you do that."

-16-

IMPORTANCE OF HEALTH INSURANCE

Adi returned home late that evening from work and his face was despaired. His mother, worried, asked him the reason for which he did not give a convincing answer and went straight into his room. When his father who returned from his walk was told about this he knocked on Adi's room and entered inside asking, "How was the day, son? Your mother was saying you didn't look too good. Is everything alright?"

"Yes, dad, I mean, no dad. My colleague Sneha's father had a heart attack this afternoon and has been hospitalized. I am coming from there. Sneha and her family are worried about his condition."

"I am sorry to hear this. How old is he?

"He is 55 years, dad. But he had been healthy I was told and suddenly he had a chest pain this afternoon and was reported as a heart attack by the doctors upon admission."

"I don't think there is anything to worry. These days medical technology has improved a lot and the doctors should fix the problem easily."

"The problem may not be only that, dad. I think they are worried about the expenses."

"Why, don't they have health insurance?"

"Unfortunately not a rupee dad. It seems nobody in their family have any medical insurance."

"What are you saying? In this age and era not having health insurance is not unfortunate, it is foolishness. What was the problem?"

"Her father was working in a private bank till recently, took voluntary retirement and is pursuing a business venture. I believe he had a family group health cover when he was in service and once he quit that benefit ceased and over the last few years they were planning to avail one, but I think they did not."

"That is the problem, Adi. People think they are invincible and immortals when they are young and don't think prudently about a future that can be unpredictable. It is imperative that every individual should be covered under health insurance adequately. You know, statistics released from the Health Ministry says that in the year 2011-12 a total of 63 million Indians were faced with poverty due to catastrophic expenditure over healthcare."

"Tell me dad, how to avoid such unpredictable happenings in life by covering under medical insurance."

"It is quite simple actually. As a thumb rule when you are below 15 years it is recommended to avail about Rs.2.00 lakhs to Rs.2.50 lakhs worth of medical insurance (sum assured) and once you are growing up it should be increased by another Rs.2 lakhs until you are 23-24 years. Then when you start working assuming your company has not covered you under group insurance add Rs.1.00 lakh more and make it Rs.5.00 lakhs."

"Can you be more specific dad?"

"Okay I shall take your example. Until you were studying and did not find a job, you would remember you had a health insurance policy of Rs.4.00 lakhs which is still continuing to be in your name. Since you are not married yet I am the proposer and I have you and your mother in the family health policy wherein both your mother, I and you are covered for a total of Rs.19 lakhs."

"Right, I remember dad, I paid the premium recently which you had given me the cheque to drop at the insurance office."

"Yes. While I am in my mid-50s, your mother is in her late 40s. In today's increasing medical costs any amount of insurance cover seems inadequate. Yet, I have covered our family of 3 for many years and though I had a group insurance cover given to me by my employer while I was working I always had a parallel medical insurance running."

"But the premiums would have been a waste, dad."

"No, I didn't consider it as a waste. In fact, I treated that as an investment for my old age."

"How dad?"

"It is not a rocket science to understand that the need for insurance cover is more as we get older and also the premiums that we pay when we are under the age of 30 are much cheaper and affordable than when we avail it when we are in our 40s, 50s or 60s. I worked in a few private companies for about 25 years before I turned a professional at my 45th year. I always knew the fact that my company covered group insurance policy was feasible only as long as I worked in those companies and once I left or changed my jobs I was vulnerable."

"Right, I think in-between jobs too could be risky phases of life."

"Absolutely son. Accidents, deaths or medical emergencies do not happen with prior intimations. It just happens. So what if I had paid premiums when I already had my company covered? Once I quit my job I continue to pay the same premium that I was paying when I was under 45 years even in my 50s now. I am actually tension-free in terms of any medical emergencies to any of my family members. In fact, now I am saving a lot more compared to those who avail health insurances late in their lives."

"But why fewer sums assured for me dad?"

"Your age, son. The chances of medical emergencies for younger people are considered less hence I had availed less against your name. Now you are old enough and once you settle down in life with your own family and commitments you too should increase it to healthy levels. I guess Rs.5.00 lacs per adult is an absolute necessity in the present times. Moreover, the medical cover comes with Cashless Facility wherein there would be no need to make payment in cash. Just showing the Health Card given by the insurance company to the hospital at the time of admission would suffice."

"Dad, had you taken this full medical cover in everybody's name in the beginning itself?"

"Actually, no. I went on topping-up the sum assured till I was 45 years with which the premiums too increased, with increase in my annual income over the years I increased my sum assured as well which now I feel is at healthy levels of Rs.7.50 lakhs each for me & your mother and Rs.4.00 lakhs for you."

"Great dad. You are a super advisor for yourself. Wish Sneha's dad too had thought about this when he was younger."

"Remember Adi, the foremost priority in life is to cover unforeseen events adequately and also to avail insurance covers when you are in your 20s than when you are in your 40s or 50s."

-17-

HOW MUCH RISK COVER IS ESSENTIAL?

"Dad, can I talk to you for a few minutes?" It was Aditya calling from his office to his dad that afternoon.

"Yes, Adi, tell me."

"Dad, I have an advisor here at my office to sign me up for an insurance plan. He says it is a pure risk cover called Term Assurance. I am slightly confused with the sum assured he is asking me to take. I wanted to seek your assistance first, that's the reason I called."

"Oh okay. You take your pen and jot down a few numbers as I speak. I shall also take my calculator, a pen and a blank sheet. Ready? Now, write down your monthly take home salary and multiply it by 12 months. Tell me what did you get?"

"Dad, I got Rs.31000 p.m. x 12 months = Rs.372000."

"Great, now divide the Rs.3.72 lakhs by 7% which would be Rs.372000 divided by 7% = Rs.53 lakhs; now this Rs.53 lakhs would be your Sum Assured for your Term Assurance insurance policy."

"Dad, wait, wait. What are you saying, I am not able to understand a thing."

"Don't get confused Adi. You are talking about a Term Assurance which is a Pure Risk Insurance Plan that covers the biggest risk of life which is "death". If a key earning member of the family prematurely dies for any reason arising out of accidents or any other reason the family will be getting into a financial mess. Through this type of an insurance plan which is designed to meet such kind of financial contingencies one can cover their risk."

"I need more clarity dad."

"Listen, under such circumstances of premature death of the main earning member of the family when he has a financially dependent family to take care, what will the surviving family members do to lead a normal life if he suddenly dies? The best way to cover this kind of an unforeseen risk is to buy an insurance plan that precisely covers this risk. In case of an untimely death the Sum Assured amount would be reimbursed by the insurance company to the legal successor or the nominee which usually would be the wife. Such amounts could be utilised by the surviving family members to lead a normal life."

"Sounds interesting dad."

"Indeed it can be interesting. I will take you as an example and will explain; see in your case......no, it is not ideal to take your example because you are just 25 and do not have significant dependants or financial commitments yet. I will consider a fictitious example of a person who is in his early 30s, married with a child and an EMI to pay."

"Okay dad, please continue."

"I will assume an individual is earning a monthly gross salary of Rs.50000, take home of Rs.45000, has household expenses of Rs.35000 including housing loan EMI of Rs.20000. In case of his sudden demise the family will find it difficult to cope with life leading to financial hardship besides emotional hardship. He could have availed a Term Assurance with a Sum Assured based on his take home monthly salary which would be: Rs.45000 x 12 / 7% = Rs.77.15 lakhs. In case of his untimely death the insurance company would pay the sum assured of Rs.77.15 lakhs to his wife, assuming she would be the nominee, which when deposited in a bank would fetch her Rs.45000 per month which is equivalent to the net salary he was bringing home when he was alive. The calculation would be: Rs.77.15 lakhs multiplied by 7% p.a. bank interest rate divided by 12 months = Rs.45000. This was the money he was utilizing for his household expenses."

"Yes, you are right dad."

"The individual has to choose his choice of sum assured either based on his Gross Income or Net Income or Mandatory Expenses that he feels is right for his family to receive as financial compensation upon his untimely death"

"The calculations are quite simple and anyone can calculate it easily. But one more doubt dad, why have you calculated at 7% as the FD interest while the current interest rates are at 9%?"

"The assumption is that the interest rates in the future may not be as high as it is today and since we cannot put a specific date for the death of a person it is better to assume a rate of interest that is lesser than today for practical calculations. So I have assumed as 7% in today's date. But in the future when you have to buy a term assurance plan you should check the prevailing risk-free interest rates and minus it by 2%. For example, two years from today if the bank interest would be 6% p.a. then take it as 4% for calculating your sum assured."

"Ok got it. Tell me about premium payments dad."

"Yes, what you have to importantly note is that under Term Assurance the premiums are not refundable in case the insured does not die during the course of the term of insurance. But if the insured dies even after paying just one premium the insurance company would compensate paying the entire sum assured to the legal successor (assumed as the wife of the insured). So naturally if the insured person survives the policy term the premiums paid would have to be treated as expense. If you calculate the outflow by way of premiums paid versus compensation received in case of death the deal seems quite good. For instance, if the sum assured is Rs.50 lakhs, premium per annum is Rs.5000 for a premium paying term of 30 years, then if the insured person does not die he would have paid Rs.5000 x 30 years = Rs.1.50 lakhs; imagine had he died, his successor would have been paid Rs.50 lakhs by the insurance firm; don't you think it is favouring the insured?

"Also the premiums are very less compared to other type of insurance plans since this type of insurance is a pure risk cover without any attachment of investment component. The premiums are pretty low at younger age and you can claim the premium for saving tax under Section 80C of the Income Tax Act.

"Further, remember that while filling the policy application form you have to mention correct information such as your age, health condition, your immediate family's health condition, do you smoke or not etc. If you hide any information or details and later it is found that such information was not provided or was falsely mentioned then your policy could be cancelled and the sum assured may not be paid. The contract becomes null & void. So be honest and give all the required information correctly and completely."

"Okay dad I fully understood. Now tell me how much sum assured should I avail?"

"See Adi, currently you need not avail full amount of sum assured. Maybe after a few years when you get married and have dependants and have some financial commitments you can take a full risk cover. Since, we, as parents are not financially dependent on you, you can take a nominal risk cover of Rs.25 lakhs and eventually once you settle down you can plan for additional risk cover. My guess is that in another 5 years you would be almost knowing how much sum assured you should consider to insure yourself for."

"Super, dad, I shall do as you say. That advisor is waiting for me for a while. I shall go and talk to him. Thanks dad, I shall see you in the evening."

FORMULA TO CALCULATE SUM ASSURED AMOUNT FOR TERM ASSURANCE:

(Assumption: The interest rate should ideally be considered 2% below the prevailing bank interest rate. For example, the prevailing interest rate in March 2015 was around 9% p.a. Hence, 7% should be considered for calculation of the sum assured. If the bank interest rate in the future goes down to 8% then 6% should be considered, so on and so forth)

ON GROSS SALARY:

Monthly Gross Salary or Income X 12 months / interest rate
(monthly gross salary or income ***multiplied*** by 12 months and ***divided*** by 7%)

Rs.50000 x 12 / 7% = Rs.85.17 lakhs (recommended sum assured) (less) existing sum assured across other existing life insurance policies such as Endowment Policy, Whole-life Policy, Money Back Policy, Unit Linked Insurance Plans or ULIP (it is assumed that you have these policies) Assuming the sum assured from these aforementioned insurance plans is Rs.15 lakhs then deduct this amount from Rs.85.17 lakhs which would be Rs.70.17 lakhs. You may round it off to Rs.70 lakhs and buy a Term Assurance Plan from any insurance company after conducting research on the premiums charged and any facilities offered. You can easily buy a term plan through online which would be quite cheap. Ideally, the Sum Assured amount for a Term Assurance Plan should be taken on Gross Salary.

INSURING HOME LOANS:

Home loans being the largest on the quantum and the longest by tenure one should definitely cover the entire loan by way of Home Loan Insurance which comes with one time premium payment and covers the entire loan amount and the tenure. A bank or housing finance company would even add the premium payable to the loan amount which can be paid by way of instalments. Most home loan companies would have tie-ups with insurance companies which should be availed without fail.

-18-

INSURANCES THAT SHOULD BE PURCHASED AND THOSE TO BE AVOIDED

"Hey Adi come here. Have you purchased the insurance plans we were discussing yet?"

"Not exactly dad, I told you there were some insurance people in my office couple of days ago, they gave away these brochures and also they were trying to explain something about various plans. In fact, I am confused dad, as there seems to be so many plans, which to buy and whether they are necessary or not I am not sure. I was thinking of checking with you about this and coincidentally you now asked me."

"Just like mutual fund companies have innumerable equity and debt schemes there are hundreds of types of insurance policies too churned out by several insurance companies, but you need to buy insurance only need based. I hope you can recall that we have discussed at length about Term Assurance and Health Insurance in the recent past which are two "must have" insurances that covers the untimely death of the main earning member of the family and the other that takes care of health related hazards. If these two are adequately taken care rest of, the investments can be done in other opportunities such as debt, equity, metal and real estate."

"Is that so dad, but I thought the insurance plans that are available in the market are all invest worthy."

"Not really, just because there is something available on a shop rack does that mean we should buy it? Like I just mentioned let it be need based. In fact, from my personal opinion we may not need to buy all the insurances that are available. We have to stick to the basics of why we need any particular insurance. Since insurance companies invest our monies that are collected by way of premiums in debt and equity markets, if we can do that on our own then we may not need their assistance for any other purposes."

"Can you please elaborate on this issue dad, I am still confused."

"See, how does the concept of the insurance work? The insured person pays an agreed premium for an agreed "sum assured" which would be compensated by the insurance company as and when the event happens. In case our vehicle gets damaged and requires repair the insurance company would pay for the charges incurred. Similarly, in case of a hospitalization the bill would be taken care by the insurance company to the maximum extent of the sum assured. Further, in case of death of the insured person the nominee or the legal successor would receive the sum assured and added benefits, if any. So, to protect my material things such as vehicle, household items, property and similar such items I shall choose to buy a "general insurance" plan that takes care of any damage that results in spending (repair charges). I would again choose the same general insurance plan to protect me from any bodily harm that results in my hospitalization. And for my death, in case it happens when I am still working, earning and having dependents, I will choose the pure risk policy that will compensate my family or survivors. Got it?"

"Sounds pretty interesting, continue dad."

"Ok. After these aspects are covered I don't think I would need any other types of protection. I shall choose to invest my rest of the funds in debt, stocks, mutual funds, gold/silver and real estate which should help me to meet all my other financial requirements."

"Is that so simple dad?"

"Simplicity comes when you are systematic with your finances and your approach. An insurance company's need would arise when you are not systematic with your finances and objectives. Since the biggest risks are death and hospitalization and if that is covered through adequate term assurance and health insurance plans why would anyone need any other amounts?"

"What about endowment plans, money-back plans, pension plans etc. which we have seen and heard enough in our lives?"

"Yeah, they have been around for a very long time and they perhaps were good plans once upon a time. But times have changed and continuing to invest in such plans today does not make sense is what I think. The overall annual returns that these kind of plans give is lesser than that of a bank recurring deposit which should be noted. Since an insurance company too invests in debt market / fixed income instruments they would be generating income based on the returns that these instruments offer. Moreover, the charges which gets deducted from the premiums that we pay may not make sense to depend on these type of plans. People used to get carried away by the fact that an assured sum would be given to the surviving family member in case of death and if survived they would get a lump sum including bonuses when they would have got older or reached retirement age. But if we calculate the returns it would have generated over the years of the policy term, the returns would have been nothing to be proud about."

"Really dad. I never knew this."

"Indeed man, the calculations tell you the real story. Since there were no big investment opportunities many years ago these plans made sense, but not today. With changing dynamics of the world and people becoming savvier with financial products they may not need such plans anymore. It would be waste of time and money. Before buying Traditional Plans such as Endowment or Money Back types of policies check the annual returns that it could generate over the tenure of the term; if it generates at least basic debt instrument returns on annualized basis then consider, if not ignore it and just buy a pure risk term plan and a health insurance plan and the rest invest systematically and religiously in different assets, you would do much better than most insurance plans.

"But, there are a few plans that may make sense such as Child Care Plans offered by insurance companies that are worth exploring. Because, the insurance company is said to plan for a child's future expenses across various events and the best thing is in case the proposer dies the rest of the premiums gets waived but the payments to the child would continue. Such insurances are worth checking out."

"Oh, that sounds to be a good plan to explore."

"Yes it could be. But the problem is insurance companies keep on designing tens of hundreds of plans and it can get confusing. So understanding and then buying them will become critical. It would be better if one checks the actual need, benefits, charges and then make a decision to buy."

"What about ULIPs dad? Are they worth?"

"I am not a big supporter of Unit Linked Insurance Plans or commonly known as ULIPs. These are a mix of insurance and mutual fund. The money collected as premium would be invested in debt and/or equity markets and the company lets the respective markets to take its own course of offering returns on the investment made. Making people to stay invested in ULIPs for a period of 10 years says it all. These were very, very expensive with some mindless and senseless charges collected on the premiums paid, wrongly sold and what not. Thankfully the charges are now reduced drastically. But if you are having a term plan that covers your death and invest on your own in debt and equity markets to meet future events then you would definitely not need buy ULIPs. That's for sure."

"Dad, any advice on Pension Plans? I think we all need some financial security by way of monthly income when we retire."

"Of course, that is the problem with retirement. We need regular and systematic funds on a monthly basis to lead our day-to-day life and by then we would have stopped working and earning. Retirement stage is also called as "passive income" stage where we try and earn income by not actively working and earning, but from our various investments. Once upon a time most government workers had the luxury of receiving pensions that would have taken care of their retirement life, but today the need of pension for everyone, particularly those who work in private companies, has become imperative. Pension Plan offered by insurance companies invest the premiums paid by us in debt and/or equity markets which would help the amounts paid by us over a longer period of time to grow to a certain extent. For example, if you were to invest Rs.25000 every year for a period of 30 years in a pension plan of an insurance company at 10% annual returns (assuming they would have invested in both equity and/or debt opportunities) it could have generated a corpus of Rs.45 lakhs. From this corpus, after 30 years every month you would be paid Rs.22500 at 6% p.a. rate of interest. This 6% is assumed which may go down (with all probability 30 years from today) and the insurance companies would alter/modify such rates in line with the prevailing market rates.

"The challenge is to decide how much pension would be enough 30 years from today to lead a normal life. Such calculations can be made with certain inflation assumptions, but difficult to arrive at an exact figure. As long as the charges on a pension plan is not exorbitant and the insurance company has assured any particular returns upon maturity of the plan then it may make sense. Check such things carefully before buying one."

"Great. I think I got to know a whole lot of things about insurance."

"There are still a lot more to learn about these, but for the time being this should be enough. Don't fall for a smart salesman's sales script and commit for any insurance. Some guys are really tricky. Always look for an advisor in a salesman, not a salesman in an advisor, they are too dangerous. Also remember, after you buy a plan and when you receive the policy document read it in detail. In case you find some aspects that are not meeting your needs or the information provided is not as per your discussion with the agent/advisor you can return the policy for cancellation, but ensure that you return it within 15 days from the date of such receipt of the policy document. It is called as "Free Look Period". The insurance company would return your premium paid and cancel the policy."

"Cool dad. Thanks a lot for such detailed explanation. That's the reason I guess you trust Prasad uncle."

"Yes, indeed. He is doing a great job with my investments. Since I too have spent adequate time in this field it becomes easier for me to understand the vagaries of investment products and precisely plan with him on my investments."

-19-

WHY DO WE NEED A FINANCIAL ADVISOR?

"Dad, my headache has not subsided still. I don't know what to do. I have already taken a day off from work."

"You should have taken some medical advice."

"Yes dad, I bought some tablets & capsules from the medical shop, but I am not able to find relief."

"Which doctor gave you the prescription? Did you see Dr.Ravindra?"

"No, dad. I did not go to any doctor. I went to the medical shop and told them my problem and the guy there gave me some tablets which I have been taking but with no respite from the splitting headache."

"Oh, there lies the problem. You did not wanted to see a "qualified" doctor but you were okay to trust a "diploma" holder to advice you on your problem. You wanted a short cut isn't it by way of saving a few hundred rupees you would have paid the doctor?"

"Not like that dad. For a small headache I thought why I should see a doctor and I went to the chemist."

"The problem was small yesterday, but today it has become big where you will have to invariably consult a doctor and perhaps even spend more money."

"Sorry dad. I should not have gone to the chemist directly."

"See Adi the issue is not about our ailments alone, we tend to tread this path of surpassing a qualified advisor even when we do our investments. We want to avoid paying any fee and do our investments in our own way or even seek advice from someone who may be a quack or fake."

"Can you be more specific dad it is sounding interesting."

"Like health is important, wealth too is important. While to maintain good health we follow certain methods of living, similarly to maintain a good wealth we need to follow healthy investing habits. We go to a gym to build our body by seeking assistance from the gym instructor who knows how to build our muscles. Exactly the same way a financial advisor too would assist us in managing our investment portfolios."

"Cool dad. I am liking your example."

"I will quote an investment example. Let's say I will buy an insurance directly from an insurance company surpassing an advisor that covers my death by saving some fee. Further, let's assume that I would die during the course of the insurance term. How would your mother and you claim that money?"

"Dad, I feel uncomfortable answering that question."

"Don't worry son, we all die one day. Answer my question."

"I guess we would go and meet the insurance company."

"Right. Do you know all the formalities that are required to get the claim? Do you think the sum assured cheque would be handed over to you across the counter?"

"Sorry dad. I am not sure about the claim process. I always thought that the settlements are done quickly."

"Settlements are not delayed intentionally, but insurance companies have to follow various procedures before they release the claim amount. You may not know all the formalities of documentation and you may have to visit the office several times. Moreover, you may not be mentally prepared to go through all such processes which would drive you into exasperation. Would you like to go through such enragement?"

"No dad, what could be the solutions for this?"

"Imagine you had engaged a good advisor to handle your investments who knows exactly how to deal under such sensitive circumstances. He or she would ensure that the settlement happens in quick time."

"Yes dad, I now understand the importance of an advisor."

"See Adi, nothing comes for free in life and it should not come for free as well. For example, you hire a taxi whose driver drives you to your destination the way you want him to drive for which you would pay him the required fee. Similarly, as an investor you should engage an advisor, pay him or her a fee and demand the kind of service you would need which would include pre-sales and post-sales as well."

"Ok dad, but how do you define a "good" and trustworthy advisor?"

"Like we trust our Dr.Ravindra whom we believe that he is worth every penny we pay him as consultation fee, we would surely find a good advisor. My friend Prasad Achaiah has been my financial advisor for over 15 years and I trust him completely. I have referred his name to many of my friends and acquaintances who too are happy with his advice as well as service. So, to get an advisor always look for good references from your close circle."

"Sure dad, I know Prasad uncle has been with you for a long time and he is doing a good job. He even helped with some of my investments. I now understood why my headache is still nagging me. I shall see Dr.Ravindra this evening and I am confident that he would be in a position to diagnose my problem and offer solutions."

"Wait son, another area of concern is people investing in mutual funds on their own. Here too an advisor's assistance is recommended. Many people buy investments without researching or invest on their own without knowing what kind of a scheme or a theme that they are investing in. These are real sins that may have destructive consequences."

"Can you elaborate dad?"

"To meet the objectives of various types of investors, mutual fund companies or asset management companies would design almost customized portfolios. For example, Franklin Templeton Mutual Fund Company has a very famous equity scheme called Franklin India Bluechip Fund which is a large-cap oriented theme that is suitable for conservative types of investors who would like to play safe with the stock market by investing in only top companies that are part of the main index such as Nifty of NSE stock exchange. Further, the same asset management company has Franklin India Prima Fund and Franklin India Flex-cap Fund that are based on mid-cap and multi-cap themes suitable for aggressive and moderately aggressive investors respectively. These are precisely designed to meet the objectives of different types of investors. An advisor would understand both aspects - customer need and the theme of the fund which would make the advisor's advisory easy."

"Nice dad. My headache seems to be receding after listening to your talk."

"I am glad of the effect Adi. Now listen, an advisor would have passed necessary mandatory exams as prescribed by the market regulator (SEBI) by making himself or herself a qualified and authorized person to advice. The advisor would be capable of understanding the nuances of such opportunities and would align it with the objectives of the investor. Out of my experience I have seen investors who do not know the difference between DSP BR Equity Fund and DSP BR T.I.G.E.R Fund; HDFC Top 200 Fund and HDFC Capital Builder Fund; Reliance Vision Fund and Reliance Growth Fund; Franklin India Bluechip Fund and Franklin India Prima Fund; ICICI Pru Dynamic Fund and ICICI Pru Value Discovery Fund. They would have invested based on various assumptions or compulsions rather than with clear understanding of the scheme and their investment objectives. Such aspects should be avoided at all cost. That is the reason the assistance of an advisor comes handy who would take care of pre-investment as well as post-investment advisory and services. It is worth is what I feel."

"Awesome dad you have made it so clear. I thought advisors were waste of time and money."

"No it is not. Pay the advisor a decent fee and demand the kind of advice and service you would need. Both of you need each other and the advisor's life depends on such advisory fee that he or she earns and I am sure today's creed of advisors are smart, intelligent and service oriented."

"Thanks dad. A simple headache made us to learn so many things and I feel so good now."

"Great. Now take rest and see if you would be meeting the doctor this evening."

-20-

HOW TO SAVE MORE?

"Adi, I hope you have started to invest in those opportunities that we discussed."

"Of course I have started investing dad. Actually I wanted to clarify about two things with you. First, how to save more so that I can invest more to meet my future requirements and second I seem to frequently have idle balances of about Rs.20000 to Rs.25000 in my savings account which I am feeling am not earning enough from my bank. Any solutions, dad?"

"I like your curiosity which is quite constructive, Adi. On the first question as to how to save more I have a question to ask if you don't mind. Can I?"

"Ask me dad, no problem."

"Do you smoke and drink?"

"Hey no dad. I don't do it. I swear, I don't."

"Great, I believe you. Why I was so blunt and personal was that, those who are smokers and drinkers spend a lot of their hard earned money on something which is neither healthy nor productive. Both of these habits are very expensive to maintain. Since generally people smoke and drink in groups it gets even more expensive. The same money they spend on these unhealthy things if they are able to save they can invest and create a handsome amount of money. Don't you think so?"

"You are bang on right dad. I am aware of it. I have been witness to many of my friends and colleagues who spend a lot of money on such parties and you very well know that I don't stay away from home beyond 7.00 pm except for my office work."

"Yes, yes, I know about you, I just asked, that's it. Please don't mind."

"No problem dad. You have all the right to question me. Please go ahead."

"Let's do some simple number calculations. Say for example, a friend of yours smokes 5 cigarettes a day, then he would be spending Rs.50 to Rs.100 per day including buying for himself and also maybe buying it for his fellow-smokers. If you multiply that for 30 days in a month then he would be spending at least Rs.3000 each month. Instead of spending on such an unhealthy habit if he invests that money in an equity mutual fund for 5 years that offers a compounded returns of just 12% per annum then he would have created a corpus of Rs.2.45 lakhs which he could perhaps use it to go on a European holiday or buy a set of Apple products. What say?"

"Wow dad. Cool. I never realized this. Actually you are right. I am sure same goes for those who drink and foot heavy bills at the bars."

"Yes, the expenses on such vices are not worth it. Moreover, as one ages the bad habits will start taking toll on the health which again leads to heavy medical bills which can be pretty expensive to manage and also irritation for the rest of the family members."

"I am glad dad that I do not have these vices."

"I am proud of you. No parents ever like to see their children smoking or drinking. It is not worth it. The only beneficiary of such habits are the companies that manufactures it and the other long term beneficiary would be doctors and hospitals."

"Now I fully understood the importance of how we should lead our lives being physically fit and also financially fit. I am sure I shall share this priceless advice with my friends and I hope that they would be taking it sportively."

"Please do it, to be good there are no age limits. Anyone can change and be good."

"Thanks dad. The other query I had, could you please clarify that?"

"Not now Adi, we have to attend a wedding and we are already late. Maybe tomorrow we shall surely discuss on your other query."

"No problem dad. Will check with you tomorrow."

-21-

MANAGING YOUR SAVINGS ACCOUNT IDLE BALANCES & BASICS OF DEBT MUTUAL FUNDS

"Dad, I seem to invariably have some idle balances quite frequently of about Rs.25000 in my savings account, I think the returns that my bank is offering is just 4% p.a. I remember you mentioning about some Liquid Funds long time ago; can you please explain me about that?"

"Well yes, I would surely let you know. First, let's know what returns does a bank offer on savings account; it is 4% p.a. based on maintaining of minimum balances in the account at the end of the month. Now, how does a bank generate a return of 4% p.a. to be passed on to their account holders? Any idea, Adi?"

"I think they utilize that money to deploy in some opportunity that generates more than 4%."

"Yes, you are right. Generally banks use such balances to deploy either in Call Money Markets where they lend to other banks that have cash deficit or invest in Reverse Repo opportunities by lending to RBI. I am sure you would have learnt about these in your college or should I refresh your memory."

"I remember dad. Call Money Market is a market where banks lend each other based on their short term funding mismatches. For example, if SBI is having some funds shortage to meet its day to day cash requirements then it would borrow from another bank, say, ICICI Bank. Similarly each of the banks do such lending and borrowing on day-to-day basis at a rate what is called as Call Rates. Am I right, dad?"

"Wow, not bad Adi, I am extremely happy that you remember what you learnt so vividly. Let me offer a bit more clarity on what you just said. Banks sit on piles of cash that it would have mobilized by way of deposits which in turn is used to offer as credit or loans to those who are in need of it. In this process of accepting deposits and lending most of the times banks would have some mismatches. For example, when Bharti Airtel bid for the 3G spectrum in 2014 it had to deposit a huge amount of money with the government. So, Bharti Airtel had to withdraw their money from the banks where they maintained their accounts. Since banks do not keep such huge funds with them all the time they would resort to borrowing from other banks to meet such sudden withdrawals who would have surplus. This is an ongoing process which happens almost daily."

"It sounds just like a businessman who manages his day to day business transactions. He borrows for a day or two and returns it once he get his funds from his other business sources."

"Exactly, only difference is that the volume of such monies are quite huge at the inter-bank level. It runs into several thousand crores. Such borrowings are done at a cost which could range from 7% p.a. to 10% p.a. where demand and supply determines the rates (prevailing rates in 2014-15). Higher demand for the funds higher would be the interest rates and a lower demand leads to lower rates. Simple rule of economics of demand and supply."

"Dad, I think those banks who are lending to other banks lend funds that they have in their savings and current accounts. Is that right?"

"Yes, almost. Those are the funds they lend and generate returns that is higher than 4%."

"Cool dad. It sounds good. And I think individuals cannot participate directly in Call Money Markets."

"Absolutely yes. Individuals cannot participate in this market. But there is a way to participate and you should know that."

"Is that Liquid Funds dad?"

"Yes, indeed, they are Liquid Funds. These are pure debt funds where a mutual fund company mobilizes funds from those who have temporary idle or surplus funds with them and deploy them in the Call Money Market through a mechanism termed as CBLO or Collateralized Borrowing & Lending Obligation. Here, in this segment RBI approved financial institutions such as mutual funds, insurance companies, provident funds, pension funds, domestic and foreign financial institutions are allowed to lend and borrow with each other which is purely based on collaterals or by offering proper security. It is a secured market and pretty safe with low risk grade."

"How does this exactly work dad?"

"See, you said you have Rs.25000 surplus in your savings account for a period of 15 days. You can invest this money in a Liquid Fund of a mutual fund company, say, HDFC Mutual Fund's Liquid Fund scheme who would mobilize funds from people quite similar to you, create a corpus and then lend it to those through the CBLO mechanism. The borrower would compensate by way of interest payment which would be earning for the mutual fund company that in turn distributes it to all the investors or unitholders."

"An example would help me to understand it better dad, please."

"Okay, here we go. You have Rs.25000 surplus in your savings account and other 999 people have same surplus with them lying idle in their banks. The total of this would be Rs.2.50 crores (Rs.25000 x 1000 people). This entire money gets mobilized by a mutual fund company which seeks opportunities in the money market through the CBLO mechanism. Let's say an insurance company is in need of short term funds for a period of 15 days to meet its urgent temporary cash shortages. The mutual fund company that has mobilized the surplus cash of Rs.2.50 crore from 1000 people would lend it to the insurance company at 8% p.a. for the required period. Upon insurance company returning the borrowed funds at the end of the fortnight the mutual fund company would have earned Rs.25000000 x 8% / 365 days x 15 days = Rs.82192. This gain would be distributed by the mutual fund company to all the 1000 investors who would get Rs.82 per investor for a period of 15 days. The transactions are done in a very systematic and organized manner under the purview of RBI."

"Oh super. But dad, only a meagre Rs.82 for 15 days?"

"Hey, come on son. Had you left the money at your bank in the savings account you would have earned just 4% and half of Rs.82 which is Rs.41. So, without sweat you are earning double. Why would you have any problem with that? And moreover, if you calculate earnings across several such opportunities in a year you would have earned a fair amount. Isn't it?"

"Oh yes. I did not think from that angle. So all such savings account balances can be invested in liquid funds? What about liquidity which my savings account offers? Would the mutual fund company let me access to the funds easily?"

"Of course. But you may not be able to withdraw cash instantly. All you should do is, plan out when you would need the cash and do the withdrawal from the fund. For example, today is 19th March and if you think you would need the money on 28th March, then you give a redemption requisition or a withdrawal request to the mutual fund company on 27th March and your money would be credited to your bank account through Direct Credit mechanism and you receive the funds on 28th March."

"It sounds cool dad. And what about any tax obligations?"

"Yeah, taxes are to be paid. On the income you earn on savings account you will have to pay taxes as per your tax slab - 10%, 20% or 30%; similarly on the income your earn on short term basis from liquid funds you will have pay as per your tax slab (short term is calculated as 3 years for debt funds). If you withdraw after 3 years you can use a facility what is termed as "indexation" which allows you the benefit of inflation adjusted returns and you may pay about 20% taxes on the gain. You can learn about this from an advisor or from Prasad Achaiah. Now listen to me carefully on the tax obligation and I am sure you will be pleasantly surprised."

"Is that so dad. Please tell me."

"On Rs.25000 at 4% p.a. for a period of 15 days you would have earned Rs.41 and let's say you come under the tax bracket of 10%, then you pay Rs.4.10 as tax and earn a post-tax income of Rs.36.90. And on the same Rs.25000 at 8% p.a. for a period of 15 days you would have earned Rs.82 and still you pay a tax of 10% which would be Rs.8.20 taking your post-tax income to Rs.73.80. Now listen, even if you have to pay 30% tax on Rs.82 still you would earn a post-tax return of Rs.57.40 which is obviously higher than Rs.36.90. How's that for some simple calculation?"

"Wow dad, it's really great. I am sure if the amount is large and am able to park my idle funds time to time my post-tax returns would be really a sizeable amount. But why doesn't everyone utilize this opportunity?"

"That is a good question Adi. Ignorance or lack of financial literacy is the reason. Our weakness is always someone else's strength. Many rich people who are generally termed as high net-worth individuals and large corporates / institutions use liquid funds regularly to park their idle funds. We all know that current account balances do not generate any returns at all. Imagine the returns on an amount of Rs.1.00 crore for a period of 15 days at 8% p.a. The pre-tax returns would be Rs.32877 for just 15 days while there would have been nil returns if continued to leave the amount in the current account of a bank. Cool isn't it?"

"Of course dad it is. I can imagine the impact now clearly. Another query dad, will the 8% p.a. returns be constant all the time?"

"Oh I forgot to tell you about that, sorry. It is a crucial question in fact. I was just giving you an example as 8% which I linked it to the prevailing Call Money rates; such rates would surely fluctuate on a daily basis. If the demand for money is high the call rates would raise and if the demand is moderate or low the rates would be lower. We can comfortably say that the returns on liquid funds is linked to the prevailing call money rates, the information which would be available in all business newspapers or RBI websites on a daily basis.

"Further, there are other pure debt funds such as Ultra Short Term Fund, Short Term Plan, Medium Term Plan and Long Term Plan in mutual funds that can be considered as an alternate for bank fixed deposits.

If one is planning to invest in a 3 year fixed deposit an Income Fund or a Gilt Fund can be considered. For investing in less than one year fixed deposit, but more than 6 months Short Term Plans would be ideal. Similarly, for parking idle funds for over 3 months, but not more than 6 months Ultra Short Term Funds are recommended. The returns would be linked to the respective debt instruments' maturity and usually they offer slightly higher returns compared to a normal bank deposit. But there would be risk associated which could be low but not completely risk-free. I am sure a good advisor can offer such opportunities of investing in debt mutual funds. The minimum amount to invest in debt mutual funds are as low as Rs.10000. It is worth trying."

"Thanks dad. I will contact Prasad uncle and request him to guide me through the investing process. I know the procedure is quite simple."

"Yes, yes. Do it. I will also put in a word to Prasad."

-22-

LOW PENETRATION INTO EQUITY INVESTING

"Dad, I keep reading news articles that says people in India are not equity savvy and they continue to prefer fixed deposits, gold, real estate and surprisingly chit funds and Ponzi schemes. Why is this trend not changed significantly despite Sensex and Nifty scaling new heights over the last 30 years?"

"See Adi, we are all victims of our social environment and upbringing. Any family hardly speaks about stock markets or mutual funds or about asset allocation based investing with their children or among themselves. Elders at home are always in a hurry to buy gold, buy multiple real estate properties and even big time participate in chit funds. The problem lies in such conditions of upbringing."

"But how will this change, dad?"

"It will change son, it is just a matter of time. Such transformation is essential and has started to happen, thanks to such efforts being put by various stakeholders of the financial services industry. The new creed of people who are in their 20s and 30s would become the ambassadors of such change because my father never knew anything about stock markets because such were the times then. Because I have been talking about equity and related stuff in the house over the years your mother too has started to understand titbits about a market which was almost non-existent till recently. As you know even your uncle - my brother has been into mutual funds for over 5 years who did not know the S of stock markets."

"Yes dad, our environment really influences us. But my doubt is beyond the knowledge about the existence of stock markets. There is a lot of misconception about this market which evidently has created infinite wealth only to a handful of investors. Why such negative perceptions?"

"I would like to attribute such perceptions related behaviour to lack of understanding of this asset class. Besides there are certain grey areas that needs to be addressed by such people who have misconceptions about the market; (1) Not defining investment objectives (2) Not having a clear understanding of which money to bring and invest in stock markets (3) Not being able to understand the dynamics of risk & return pay-offs (4) Comparing this asset class with other asset classes which are quite different across various parameters (5) Not giving another chance after any losses (6) Herd mentality (7) Not investing on learning (8) Having impractical expectations about the returns that stock markets could generate (9) Not disciplined and systematic (10) Will panic too easily."

"Wow, so many grey areas?"

"Of course Adi and given a chance I would add a few more. It is like the idiom "everyone wants to go to heaven, but nobody wants to die". When it comes to investments too most of the people are in a hurry to make higher returns, but do not want to understand the risk dynamics. For example, if you have to travel a distance of 500 kms in 10 hours you will travel at a speed of 50 kms per hour, but if you would like to reach in 5 hours you will have to increase the speed, so with higher speed risk too increases. It is as simple actually."

"True dad. I come to understand now that if I want higher return I should be ready to take risk."

"Indeed son. While buying a car we conduct meticulous research, we don't buy a car in one day. In fact, by the time we finally drive a car out from a showroom it would have taken several weeks because we would have spent so much time on researching on various aspects about the car. Similarly, even when a saree is bought so much research goes behind it. Ask your mother, she will tell her experiences of buying sarees. But when it comes to investing in equities such painstaking work is missing. Why? If I have made good gains being an investor over the years, why not others?"

"Yes, dad. I remember you mentioning that you have made good returns on your investments in stocks and mutual funds."

"Stock markets are not Jurassic Park as perceived by many. It is a place of opportunities. With decent amount of time and energy spent on learning simple things about the companies that are listed on stock exchanges I wonder why anyone would make losses. Of course, losses may happen, it is part of all investments. With a good diversification mechanism even losses can be addressed without sweat."

"So what is the simple advice dad?"

"See, during March 2015 the Reserve Bank of India reduced the interest rates which led the banks to reduce the interest rates on fixed deposits. The one year fixed deposit and recurring deposit rates which were in the range of 9% per annum till then started to come down in line with the key rate reduction. Which means as the risk-free interest rates start coming down the ability to create wealth too starts coming down. People would start finding it difficult to depend on bank deposits or post office savings instruments to achieve higher returns. They would have to start embracing risky investments or risky asset classes. Let's not forget the fact that millions of people in our country still believe in Chit Funds, Unorganized Financial Sector such as private finances to achieve their financial goals. The same risk that they are taking can be shifted to equity markets by way of investing in stocks or mutual funds. Stock Markets are part of Organized Financial Sector which has a world class regulator in the form of SEBI. All one would need is seeking knowledge of how this market operates and the procedures to manage risk and achieve higher or inflation beating returns. It is not rocket science either."

"Very true dad. I think people have to start changing their mind-sets and transformation is the key."

"Another saddest part of this system is most Chartered Accountants or Auditors who are actually quite qualified individuals seldom advice their clients to invest their money in equities as part of the Tax Saving opportunity such as ELSS or Equity Linked Saving Scheme. It is really baffling. These aspects have to change and a transformation is essential.

"Further, achieving higher returns are not easy. No pain, no gain. Define your returns objective as to how much returns you are expecting and if your expectations are practical......"

"Wow, wait dad. What is this "practical" expectations of returns?"

"Practical means, not to expect extraordinary returns or abnormal returns. For example, I should not buy a stock with the expectation of doubling my investment in one year. That approach would be wrong."

"But dad, I have heard and also literally seen that many stocks have actually given 100% returns in a short time. So why not?"

"That's the wrong approach I am saying son. Every time you cannot expect Virat Kohli to score a century when he is on the field; you cannot expect Roger Federer to win all grand slams. It is not practical approach. Sometimes Kohli may score back-to-back centuries, Federer may win back-to-back matches, but can they repeat it innings after innings, match after match?"

"Obviously not."

"Sometimes such returns do happen, that's why I keep telling you that equity market offers infinite opportunities. It is all about how a stock or the prospects of a company is perceived by larger public who are part of the equity market in a given time. But, such examples should not be construed as it would be an ongoing possibility of making exorbitant returns all the time."

"So then, what should be practical expectation of returns?"

"I guess, about 15% annual return on compounded basis is a good practical expectation."

"Any thumb rule for this expectation?"

"Yeah you can use the word thumb rule here because if the fixed income products such as post office savings and bank deposits are offering returns of 8% to 9% per annum, then achieving returns in the range of 15% from equities year on year sounds a very practical approach. A single stock or a single mutual fund scheme may actually offer us unbelievable returns, but that should not be the criteria for investing. Returns should be achieved as a portfolio of stocks or mutual funds, then if we expect 15% returns on year-on-year basis it would be practical is what I profess."

"Sounds cool dad. I too think a portfolio sounds very professional method of investing."

"Indeed, I have elaborately discussed such possibilities in the past with you; a portfolio based investing is the best method of investing. Also people who are not in a position to do research on specific sector or stock before investing they can simply choose mutual funds to invest. Mutual funds offer a great indirect entry opportunity to stock markets."

"I too feel the same dad."

"Yes, yes. You should largely stick to mutual funds, I think I have already spoken with you about mutual funds in the past."

"Another thing dad, many people think and worry about the index (Nifty or Sensex) or the overall market all the time thinking that markets are high or low. Is it the correct method of deciding to invest?"

"Let me ask you a question before I answer this query of yours. When you are driving a car do you look at the speedo-meter and drive or look at the road and drive?"

"Dad, it is a pretty silly question. Obviously I would be looking at the road and driving and intermittently maybe I would look at the speedo-meter."

"Ah, you said it! Index is like the speedo-meter and Market is like the road. We should be concentrating on the market not on the index. You go on and buy stocks or mutual funds and stay invested to meet your investment goal; intermittently you check the index to find out if there is anything wrong and then take some corrective steps by revising your portfolio. If you keep on thinking about the index you would miss the market. So use some common sense while investing and staying invested."

"Wow, dad. I never had thought about markets in this manner. You are so right with the example."

"These are simple aspects which many ignore. There is a lot of negative awareness about equity market which needs to be addressed. Only those who have no idea about market make such nasty remarks. Let's snub these type of people from our lives and start getting knowledgeable and be "investment literates."

"Surely dad, with your guidance from time to time I too would be called as an "informed investor."

"That's pretty progressive aspiration son."

-23-

IS INVESTING IN EQUITIES REALLY RISKY?

The objective of all investments is to earn profits at a future date. As an investment asset equity (stocks & mutual funds) has the worst tag of being the riskiest of all compared to other asset classes such as debt, gold and real estate. Does equity deserve such a tag? Let's consider a few risky options which are part of our daily lives:

- Parents invest in their children by educating them (for about 17 years, let's not forget the time invested) under the "assumption" that the children will grow up as educated individuals and will be able to find jobs, will be able to stand on their own feet and maybe take care of them when they get older. Can the parents be 100% sure of the success of their investment? Still parents "invest" time and money on their children with conviction.
- A girl marries a boy (and vice versa is also true) under the "assumption" that she/he will live happily ever after with that person. Can the girl or boy be 100% sure of this? Yet, marriages continue to happen.
- A wife conceives to have a child some 9 months from a doctor-confirmed date. The husband invests in the nourishment of the mother (and the to-be-born child) under the "assumption" that a healthy child will be born. Can the husband & wife be 100% sure of delivering a healthy child? On an average 4 kids are born every second world over.
- A father sends his daughter / son for a sport, pays fees, buys a lot of ancillary sports related stuff in an "assumption" that the

kid will become at least a state-level player. Can the father be 100% sure of the child being a famous sports person?

- A homemaker woman buys a flower plant and expects the plant to give flowers in the days to come and she waters it, nourishes it carefully. Can she be 100% sure of the plant growing healthily and give flowers?
- A player is bought by an IPL (Indian Premier League T20 cricket team) franchisee owner paying a handsome price under the assumption that he will be a star performer in the next season. Can the owner be 100% sure of the performance from his purchase? (How can we forget the episode of Sreesanth, a promising cricketer, who was purchased by the franchisee Rajasthan Royals?)

If the answer is that you are not 100% sure for any of the above "assumptions" then you should definitely not say equity markets are the riskiest. It is just one of the assets that is risky and the assumptions are similar to that of any other routine events of our lives.

Infosys was a new and unheard company in 1993 when people did not know that over the future technology would rule the world. So was Wipro, TCS, Havells, Colgate, Maruti Suzuki, Asian Paints, Lupin, Yes Bank among many other companies which have created astonishing wealth over the years. Once upon a time these companies were new with a lot of "assumptions" if they would do well given the fact that the market was fraught with so many challenges and uncertainties.

Just like a pregnant woman who goes through pain, fear and uncertainty yet delivers a healthy baby (well, in most cases), a company too goes through similar process. If her husband, her parents, her in-laws, her siblings, her friends supports her and encourages her through the nine months of her pregnancy such handholding, warmth, support and assurance is needed for companies too to deliver outstanding performances. It is a challenging environment out there in the market place to be successful and build a name, brand and reputation.

Like all pregnant women cannot deliver 100% healthy babies, like all children may not grow up to become successful, like all plants may not offer fruits and flowers, like all sportsmen cannot become Tendulkar or Federer or Schumacher, investing in companies too cannot lead to 100% successful investments. There would be exceptions which is part of any investment. Companies fail despite sincere efforts or maybe there was not enough effort put (many of us keep saying: if I had been given good opportunities I too would have become successful). For a product to be accepted by a customer it needs a lot of investment besides money alone; time, effort, innovation, competition and what not......

Let's not forget that the batting legend Sachin Tendulkar had to play 79 one day innings before he scored his first century. Someone in the cricket control board supported or had faith in his abilities; if not we would have missed watching such a legendary player's cricketing finesse who went on to record highest number of runs in all formats of the game.

Yes, life is full of risks and risk is inherent in every aspect of our life. When we invest in a company we are going through the same level of intensity of risk that prevails or exists in many other aspects of our daily lives. Let's not be cynical and keep blaming the equity market that it is risky. It is risky, but look at the pay-offs. Hundreds of companies over the last few decades have offered some unbelievable returns to investors who believed in such possibilities.

Companies like Satyam Computers, Kingfisher Airlines and a few others have failed miserably and made investors poorer, but such lessons are essential for investors and the regulators to be warned of such possibilities. The fact that Satyam Computers failed helped the regulator to tighten the screws of corporate governance which set a benchmark for all other companies; and the fact that Kingfisher Airlines failed the lenders learnt a lesson or two about their lending parameters. But let such experiences not deter us from not believing in the system of stock markets. It is part of the organized financial markets and reforms are an ongoing process.

If the idea of having more than one child, having more than one plant in a garden, having more than one bank account, keeping two pens in the pocket etc. can be diversification then investing in multiple assets, multiple stocks, multiple mutual funds too is diversification that reduces risk.

Risk mitigation is simple; one has to adapt and be adept. Let's not have a negative opinion of an asset about which we have no in-depth knowledge at all. Let's pledge to learn and be called as "financial literates" and begin our journey as "informed investors" and not as "prejudiced investors."

PART 2

COMPLEMENTARY ATTACHMENTS INDEX

<u>PAGE 134</u>: MUTUAL FUND PORTFOLIO CONSTRUCTION IDEAS (investor suitability of mutual fund themes based on their risk profiles)

<u>PAGE 135</u>: MUTUAL FUND PORTFOLIOS BASED ON RISK PROFILES (portfolio construction ideas based on the themes across different types of investor profiles with recommended weights)

<u>PAGES 136 to 138</u>: MODEL MUTUAL FUND PORTFOLIOS (Model mutual fund portfolios across conservative, moderately aggressive & aggressive type investors)

<u>PAGES 139 to 144</u>: FRANKLIN INDIA BLUECHIP FUND (a Large Cap oriented scheme) SIP PERFORMANCE FROM THE MONTH OF ITS LAUNCH IN 1993 TILL DECEMBER 2014 (A monthly investment amount of Rs.1000 invested for 252 months totaling to Rs.2.52 lakhs (principal amount) growing to become Rs.25.47 lakhs in 21 years offering compounded returns of approx. 17% p.a.)

<u>PAGES 145 to 150</u>: FRANKLIN INDIA PRIMA FUND (a Mid-Cap oriented scheme) SIP PERFORMANCE FROM THE MONTH OF ITS LAUNCH IN 1993 TILL DECEMBER 2014 (A monthly investment amount of Rs.1000 invested for 252 months totaling to Rs.2.52 lakhs (principal amount) growing to become Rs.50.13 lakhs in 21 years offering compounded returns of approx. 22% p.a.)

<u>PAGES 151 to 156</u>: HDFC EQUITY FUND (A Large & Mid-cap oriented scheme) SIP PERFORMANCE FROM THE MONTH OF ITS LAUNCH IN JANUARY 1995 TILL DECEMBER 2014 (A monthly investment amount of Rs.1000 invested for 240 months totaling to Rs.2.40 lakhs (principal amount) growing to become Rs.50.52 lakhs in 20 years offering compounded returns of approx. 23% p.a.)

<u>PAGES 157 to 162</u>: HDFC PRUDENCE FUND (A Balanced Fund) SIP PERFORMANCE FROM THE MONTH OF ITS LAUNCH IN FEBRUARY 1994 TILL DECEMBER 2014 (A monthly investment amount of Rs.1000 invested for 252 months totaling to Rs.2.52 lakhs (principal amount) growing

to become Rs.37.66 lakhs in 21 years offering compounded returns of approx. 20% p.a.)

PAGE 163: SYSTEMATIC INVESTMENT PLAN or SIP INVESTMENT MODEL PORTFOLIOS (choosing a portfolio route to invest in SIPs across different types of investor profiles)

PAGE 164: MUTUAL FUND THEME DIFFERENTIATOR CHART (different themes offering different returns that are designed to meet the risk profiles; conservative to moderately aggressive to aggressive types of themes that proves that each scheme is designed to meet a specific purpose or objective of investors)

PAGE 165: EDUCATION INFLATION @ 7.50% (an indicative chart that defines the future education costs based on present costs assuming at an annual inflation rate of 7.50%; this is the money that parents may have to spend on their kid's education)

INDICATIVE INVESTOR RISK PROFILES	
Returns Range (per annum basis)	**Type of Investors**
FD based returns	Ultra Conservative
9% to 12%	Conservative
12% to 15%	Moderately Conservative
15% to 18%	Moderately Aggressive
18% to 25%	Aggressive
25% & above	Ultra Aggressive
Note: 9% returns has been considered as base fixed deposit returns on one year rates, prevailing during 2014-15 at leading PSU and private banks	

INDICATIVE TIME HORIZON OF INVESTING BASED ON EVENTS	
Time Range	**Classification**
1 day to 3 months	Ultra Short Term
3 months to 1 year	Short Term
1 year to 3 years	Medium Term
3 years to 10 years	Long Term
10 years & above	Ultra Long Term
Note: The range is based on liquidity requirements of aspiring investors. The range is only indicative that is to have clarity on objectives of staying invested to meet them. Such period may vary from investor to investor.	

Gold ETF (listed on National Stock Exchange)			
Date of Invt.	Per Unit Price (Rs.)	Invt. Amt	Units
13-Apr-07	948	1000.00	1.054
10-May-07	911	1000.00	1.098
11-Jun-07	875	1000.00	1.142
10-Jul-07	875	1000.00	1.143
10-Aug-07	884	1000.00	1.131
10-Sep-07	934	1000.00	1.071
10-Oct-07	950	1000.00	1.052
12-Nov-07	1046	1000.00	0.956
10-Dec-07	1025	1000.00	0.976
10-Jan-08	1115	1000.00	0.897
11-Feb-08	1192	1000.00	0.839
10-Mar-08	1281	1000.00	0.781
10-Apr-08	1204	1000.00	0.830
9-May-08	1189	1000.00	0.841
10-Jun-08	1232	1000.00	0.812
10-Jul-08	1299	1000.00	0.770
11-Aug-08	1191	1000.00	0.840
10-Sep-08	1147	1000.00	0.872
10-Oct-08	1368	1000.00	0.731
10-Nov-08	1157	1000.00	0.864
10-Dec-08	1235	1000.00	0.810
9-Jan-09	1315	1000.00	0.761
10-Feb-09	1385	1000.00	0.722
9-Mar-09	1525	1000.00	0.656
13-Apr-09	1420	1000.00	0.704
11-May-09	1444	1000.00	0.693
10-Jun-09	1456	1000.00	0.687
10-Jul-09	1432	1000.00	0.698
10-Aug-09	1473	1000.00	0.679
10-Sep-09	1547	1000.00	0.647
12-Oct-09	1578	1000.00	0.634
10-Nov-09	1646	1000.00	0.607

Mutual Fund SIP (HDFC Equity Fund)			
Date of Invt.	NAV (Rs.)	Invt. Amt (Rs.)	Units
10-Apr-07	144.48	1000.00	6.922
10-May-07	149.40	1000.00	6.693
11-Jun-07	158.85	1000.00	6.295
10-Jul-07	169.19	1000.00	5.911
10-Aug-07	166.58	1000.00	6.003
10-Sep-07	172.50	1000.00	5.797
10-Oct-07	189.83	1000.00	5.268
12-Nov-07	199.97	1000.00	5.001
10-Dec-07	213.45	1000.00	4.685
10-Jan-08	220.01	1000.00	4.545
11-Feb-08	177.14	1000.00	5.645
11-Mar-08	175.11	1000.00	5.711
10-Apr-08	166.00	1000.00	6.024
12-May-08	173.29	1000.00	5.771
10-Jun-08	158.62	1000.00	6.305
10-Jul-08	146.89	1000.00	6.808
11-Aug-08	164.53	1000.00	6.078
10-Sep-08	162.47	1000.00	6.155
10-Oct-08	117.70	1000.00	8.496
10-Nov-08	117.67	1000.00	8.498
10-Dec-08	106.56	1000.00	9.385
12-Jan-09	106.00	1000.00	9.434
10-Feb-09	106.97	1000.00	9.348
12-Mar-09	93.42	1000.00	10.704
13-Apr-09	121.22	1000.00	8.250
11-May-09	131.38	1000.00	7.611
10-Jun-09	178.02	1000.00	5.617
10-Jul-09	163.24	1000.00	6.126
10-Aug-09	179.00	1000.00	5.587
10-Sep-09	196.46	1000.00	5.090
12-Oct-09	216.44	1000.00	4.620
10-Nov-09	221.24	1000.00	4.520

Bank Recurring Deposit	
Date of Invt.	Invt. Amt (Rs.)
10-Apr-07	1000.00
10-May-07	1000.00
11-Jun-07	1000.00
10-Jul-07	1000.00
10-Aug-07	1000.00
10-Sep-07	1000.00
10-Oct-07	1000.00
12-Nov-07	1000.00
10-Dec-07	1000.00
10-Jan-08	1000.00
11-Feb-08	1000.00
11-Mar-08	1000.00
10-Apr-08	1000.00
12-May-08	1000.00
10-Jun-08	1000.00
10-Jul-08	1000.00
11-Aug-08	1000.00
10-Sep-08	1000.00
10-Oct-08	1000.00
10-Nov-08	1000.00
10-Dec-08	1000.00
12-Jan-09	1000.00
10-Feb-09	1000.00
12-Mar-09	1000.00
13-Apr-09	1000.00
11-May-09	1000.00
10-Jun-09	1000.00
10-Jul-09	1000.00
10-Aug-09	1000.00
10-Sep-09	1000.00
12-Oct-09	1000.00
10-Nov-09	1000.00

Gold ETF (listed on National Stock Exchange)			
Date of Invt.	Per Unit Price (Rs.)	Invt. Amt	Units
10-Dec-09	1687	1000.00	0.593
11-Jan-10	1680	1000.00	0.595
10-Feb-10	1607	1000.00	0.622
10-Mar-10	1646	1000.00	0.608
12-Apr-10	1658	1000.00	0.603
10-May-10	1708	1000.00	0.585
10-Jun-10	1838	1000.00	0.544
12-Jul-10	1807	1000.00	0.553
10-Aug-10	1778	1000.00	0.562
9-Sep-10	1866	1000.00	0.536
11-Oct-10	1913	1000.00	0.523
10-Nov-10	1985	1000.00	0.504
10-Dec-10	1998	1000.00	0.501
10-Jan-11	1974	1000.00	0.507
10-Feb-11	1971	1000.00	0.507
10-Mar-11	2044	1000.00	0.489
11-Apr-11	2067	1000.00	0.484
10-May-11	2148	1000.00	0.465
10-Jun-11	2183	1000.00	0.458
11-Jul-11	2168	1000.00	0.461
10-Aug-11	2493	1000.00	0.401
12-Sep-11	2707	1000.00	0.369
10-Oct-11	2543	1000.00	0.393
11-Nov-11	2742	1000.00	0.365
12-Dec-11	2752	1000.00	0.363
10-Jan-12	2635	1000.00	0.379
10-Feb-12	2684	1000.00	0.373
12-Mar-12	2674	1000.00	0.374
10-Apr-12	2689	1000.00	0.372
10-May-12	2723	1000.00	0.367
11-Jun-12	2823	1000.00	0.354
10-Jul-12	2813	1000.00	0.356
10-Aug-12	2842	1000.00	0.352
10-Sep-12	3063	1000.00	0.326

Mutual Fund SIP (HDFC Equity Fund)			
Date of Invt.	NAV (Rs.)	Invt. Amt (Rs.)	Units
10-Dec-09	228.69	1000.00	4.373
11-Jan-10	234.50	1000.00	4.264
10-Feb-10	219.46	1000.00	4.557
10-Mar-10	230.48	1000.00	4.339
12-Apr-10	239.03	1000.00	4.184
10-May-10	238.81	1000.00	4.187
10-Jun-10	243.89	1000.00	4.100
12-Jul-10	257.36	1000.00	3.886
10-Aug-10	267.80	1000.00	3.734
13-Sep-10	287.10	1000.00	3.483
11-Oct-10	300.19	1000.00	3.331
10-Nov-10	312.19	1000.00	3.203
10-Dec-10	289.22	1000.00	3.458
10-Jan-11	282.22	1000.00	3.543
10-Feb-11	256.55	1000.00	3.898
10-Mar-11	267.14	1000.00	3.743
11-Apr-11	284.25	1000.00	3.518
10-May-11	278.81	1000.00	3.587
10-Jun-11	277.24	1000.00	3.607
11-Jul-11	281.27	1000.00	3.555
10-Aug-11	262.56	1000.00	3.809
12-Sep-11	245.47	1000.00	4.074
10-Oct-11	244.04	1000.00	4.098
11.11.11	246.75	1000.00	4.053
12.12.11	228.95	1000.00	4.368
10.01.12	229.09	1000.00	4.365
10.02.12	260.84	1000.00	3.834
12.03.12	264.00	1000.00	3.788
10.04.12	259.16	1000.00	3.859
10.05.12	242.47	1000.00	4.124
11.06.12	247.97	1000.00	4.033
10.07.12	262.17	1000.00	3.814
10.08.12	253.28	1000.00	3.948
10.09.12	255.33	1000.00	3.917

Bank Recurring Deposit	
Date of Invt.	Invt. Amt (Rs.)
10-Dec-09	1000.00
11-Jan-10	1000.00
10-Feb-10	1000.00
10-Mar-10	1000.00
12-Apr-10	1000.00
10-May-10	1000.00
10-Jun-10	1000.00
12-Jul-10	1000.00
10-Aug-10	1000.00
13-Sep-10	1000.00
11-Oct-10	1000.00
10-Nov-10	1000.00
10-Dec-10	1000.00
10-Jan-11	1000.00
10-Feb-11	1000.00
10-Mar-11	1000.00
11-Apr-11	1000.00
10-May-11	1000.00
10-Jun-11	1000.00
11-Jul-11	1000.00
10-Aug-11	1000.00
12-Sep-11	1000.00
10-Oct-11	1000.00
11.11.11	1000.00
12.12.11	1000.00
10.01.12	1000.00
10.02.12	1000.00
12.03.12	1000.00
10.04.12	1000.00
10.05.12	1000.00
11.06.12	1000.00
10.07.12	1000.00
10.08.12	1000.00
10.09.12	1000.00

Gold ETF (listed on National Stock Exchange)			
Date of Invt.	Per Unit Price (Rs.)	Invt. Amt	Units
10-Oct-12	2980	1000.00	0.336
9-Nov-12	3015	1000.00	0.332
10-Dec-12	2962	1000.00	0.338
10-Jan-13	2884	1000.00	0.347
11-Feb-13	2884	1000.00	0.347
11-Mar-13	2779	1000.00	0.360
10-Apr-13	2785	1000.00	0.359
10-May-13	2577	1000.00	0.388
10-Jun-13	2608	1000.00	0.383
10-Jul-13	2482	1000.00	0.403
12-Aug-13	2708	1000.00	0.369
10-Sep-13	2824	1000.00	0.354
10-Oct-13	2841	1000.00	0.352
11-Nov-13	2866	1000.00	0.349
10-Dec-13	2830	1000.00	0.353
10-Jan-14	2752	1000.00	0.363
10-Feb-14	2791	1000.00	0.358
10-Mar-14	2805	1000.00	0.357
10-Apr-14	2710	1000.00	0.369
9-May-14	2764	1000.00	0.362
10-Jun-14	2470	1000.00	0.405
10-Jul-14	2634	1000.00	0.380
11-Aug-14	2620	1000.00	0.382
10-Sep-14	2525	1000.00	0.396
10-Oct-14	2486	1000.00	0.402
10-Nov-14	2412	1000.00	0.415
10-Dec-14	2486	1000.00	0.402
Investment Amount & Units		93000.00	52.801
Value with growth			131263.51
CAGR			8.55%

Mutual Fund SIP (HDFC Equity Fund)			
Date of Invt.	NAV (Rs.)	Invt. Amt (Rs.)	Units
10.10.12	276.83	1000.00	3.612
09.11.12	275.78	1000.00	3.626
10.12.12	291.43	1000.00	3.431
10.01.13	299.26	1000.00	3.342
11.02.13	288.71	1000.00	3.464
11.03.13	286.04	1000.00	3.496
11.04.13	269.76	1000.00	3.707
10-May-13	289.02	1000.00	3.460
10-Jun-13	278.47	1000.00	3.591
10-Jul-13	266.16	1000.00	3.757
12-Aug-13	248.31	1000.00	4.027
10-Sep-13	260.72	1000.00	3.836
10-Oct-13	269.15	1000.00	3.715
10-Nov-13	282.70	1000.00	3.537
10-Dec-13	299.96	1000.00	3.334
10-Jan-14	295.82	1000.00	3.380
10-Feb-14	289.92	1000.00	3.449
10-Mar-14	318.89	1000.00	3.136
10-Apr-14	342.44	1000.00	2.920
9-May-14	353.48	1000.00	2.829
10-Jun-14	422.22	1000.00	2.368
10-Jul-14	416.56	1000.00	2.401
11-Aug-14	418.12	1000.00	2.392
10-Sep-14	454.45	1000.00	2.200
10-Oct-14	439.62	1000.00	2.275
10-Nov-14	468.81	1000.00	2.133
10-Dec-14	471.27	1000.00	2.122
Investment Amount & Units		93000.00	427.0761242
Value with growth			201268.17
CAGR			18.18%

Bank Recurring Deposit	
Date of Invt.	Invt. Amt (Rs.)
10.10.12	1000.00
09.11.12	1000.00
10.12.12	1000.00
10.01.13	1000.00
11.02.13	1000.00
11.03.13	1000.00
11.04.13	1000.00
10-May-13	1000.00
10-Jun-13	1000.00
10-Jul-13	1000.00
12-Aug-13	1000.00
10-Sep-13	1000.00
10-Oct-13	1000.00
10-Nov-13	1000.00
10-Dec-13	1000.00
10-Jan-14	1000.00
10-Feb-14	1000.00
10-Mar-14	1000.00
10-Apr-14	1000.00
9-May-14	1000.00
10-Jun-14	1000.00
10-Jul-14	1000.00
11-Aug-14	1000.00
10-Sep-14	1000.00
10-Oct-14	1000.00
10-Nov-14	1000.00
10-Dec-14	1000.00
Invt. Amount	93000.00
Value with growth	137698.00
CAGR	8.50%

Note: The above compilation of data is to prove that asset allocation based investing would be the best way to achieve inflation beating returns. The period taken is from April 2007 since that is month Gold ETF was introduced on National Stock Exchange. It is further assumed that had Rs.1000 been invested in Gold, Diversified Equity Mutual Fund and Bank Recurring Deposit for a period of 93 months ending in Dec 2014 from April 2007 then the returns across all three investments with equal distribution of amounts would have given an average returns of 11.74% which would have been enough to beat the inflation over these months/years. CAGR is Compounded Annualized Gross Return; basically is compounded returns over the given period of time.

SELECT STOCKS' PERFORMANCE IN 10 YEARS (FEB 2005 to FEB 2015); PRODUCTS OR SERVICES OF THESE WHICH WE WOULD HAVE USED

Company Name	Industry	No. of shares in 2005	Price in Feb 2005	Invt. Cost in 2005	Price in Feb 2015	No. of shares in 2015	Invt. Value in 2015	Compounded Returns in 10 years
ASIAN PAINTS	Paints	100	335.00	33500.00	800.00	1000 (stock split)	800000.00	37.34%
BATA INDIA	Retail	100	93.00	9300.00	1250.00	100	125000.00	29.67%
BLUEDART	Logistics & Courier	100	332.00	33200.00	6800.00	100	680000.00	35.25%
CANFIN HOMES	Financial Services (home loan)	100	46.00	4600.00	602.00	100	60200.00	29.33%
COLGATE	FMCG	100	187.00	18700.00	1973.00	100	197300.00	26.57%
CRISIL	Financial Services (credit rating)	100	535.00	53500.00	2025.00	1000 (stock split)	2025000.00	43.82%
DEWAN HOUSING FINANCE	Financial Services (home loan)	100	33.00	3300.00	502.00	100	50200.00	31.29%
EICHER MOTORS	Automobile	100	270.00	27000.00	16000.00	100	1600000.00	50.41%
GODREJ CONSUMER	Consumer Durables	100	278.00	27800.00	1120.00	400 (stock split)	448000.00	32.05%
HAVELLS INDIA	Electrical Equipments	100	258.00	25800.00	275.00	4000 (bonus & stock split)	1100000.00	45.54%
JUNIORBEES	Index ETF	100	43.00	4300.00	195.00	100	19500.00	16.32%
NIFTYBEES	Index ETF	100	210.00	21000.00	879.00	100	87900.00	15.39%
MARUTI SUZUKI	Automobile	100	449.00	44900.00	3600.00	100	360000.00	23.14%
PIDILITE INDS.	Chemicals (Fevicol mfg. co)	100	408.00	40800.00	563.00	2000 (bonus & stock split)	1126000.00	39.34%
TITAN Co.	Retail	100	178.00	17800.00	422.00	2000 (bonus & stock split)	844000.00	37.09%
TTK PRESTIGE	Consumer Durables	100	36.00	3600.00	3188.00	100	318800.00	56.57%

Note: The above examples of stocks/ETFs prove a point that not only renowned / bluechip companies such as Infosys, TCS, Wipro, SBI, Reliance, ACC can offer great returns, there are many other companies other than the tried and tested stocks whose products we would have consumed or purchased regularly can offer amazing returns. Despite equity markets being risky, choppy and uncertain, if we use a bit of common sense and conduct some research, we can indeed achieve inflation beating returns and more from the equity markets.

BSE 500 INDICES STOCK CLASSIFICATION - COMPANY, SECTOR, INDUSTRY & MARKET CAPITALIZATION (as on December 2014)				
COMPANY	SECTOR	INDUSTRY	Full Market Cap (in crore)	Market Cap Category
Kaveri Seed Company Ltd.	Agriculture	Other Agri products	5474.84	Large Cap
Amara Raja Batteries Ltd.	Automobile	Batteries	13743.57	Large Cap
Amtek Auto Ltd.	Automobile	Auto Ancillaries	3727.78	Mid Cap
Amtek India Ltd.	Automobile	Auto Ancillaries	1866.48	Small Cap
Apollo Tyres Ltd.	Automobile	Tyres & Tubes	11351.25	Large Cap
Ashok Leyland Ltd.	Automobile	Commercial Vehicles	14599.35	Large Cap
Bajaj Auto Ltd	Automobile	Two & Three Wheelers	72024.9	Mega Cap
Balkrishna Industries Ltd.	Automobile	Tyres & Tubes	5798.07	Large Cap
Bharat Forge Ltd.	Automobile	Auto Ancillaries	21900.13	Large Cap
Bosch Ltd.	Automobile	Auto Ancillaries	60680.57	Mega Cap
Castrol India Ltd.	Automobile	Lubricants, etc.	24750.31	Large Cap
Ceat Ltd.	Automobile	Tyres & Tubes	3435.63	Mid Cap
Eicher Motors Ltd.	Automobile	Commercial Vehicles	41627.84	Large Cap
Escorts Ltd.	Automobile	Auto Ancillaries	1583.69	Small Cap
Exide Industries Ltd.	Automobile	Storage Batteries	14998.25	Large Cap
Hero Motocorp Ltd.	Automobile	Two & Three Wheelers	62918.54	Mega Cap
HMT Ltd.	Automobile	Auto Ancillaries	3558.44	Mid Cap
JK Tyre & Industries Ltd.	Automobile	Tyres & Tubes	2670.91	Mid Cap
Kirloskar Oil Engines Ltd.	Automobile	Auto Ancillaries	3887.94	Mid Cap
Mahindra & Mahindra Ltd.	Automobile	Cars & Multi Utility Vehicles	77735.92	Mega Cap
Maruti Suzuki India Ltd.	Automobile	Cars & Multi Utility Vehicles	101098.64	Mega Cap
Motherson Sumi Systems Ltd.	Automobile	Auto Ancillaries	39554.08	Large Cap
MRF Ltd.	Automobile	Tyres & Tubes	16261.56	Large Cap
Sundram Fasteners Ltd.	Automobile	Auto Ancillaries	3815.93	Mid Cap
Tata Motors Ltd.	Automobile	Commercial Vehicles	135453.62	Mega Cap
Tube Investments Of India Ltd.	Automobile	Auto Ancillaries	6746.82	Large Cap
TVS Motor Co. Ltd.	Automobile	Two & Three Wheelers	12832.1	Large Cap
Wabco India Ltd.	Automobile	Auto Ancillaries	8856.44	Large Cap
Jet Airways India Ltd	Aviation	Air Transport	4323.52	Mid Cap
Allahabad Bank	Banking	PSU Bank	7041.8	Large Cap
Andhra Bank	Banking	PSU Bank	5291.79	Large Cap
Bank Of Baroda	Banking	PSU Bank	45893.74	Large Cap
Bank of India	Banking	PSU Bank	19245.41	Large Cap
Bank of Maharashtra	Banking	PSU Bank	4444.1	Mid Cap
Canara Bank	Banking	PSU Bank	20424.54	Large Cap
Central Bank of India	Banking	PSU Bank	12772.31	Large Cap
Corporation Bank	Banking	PSU Bank	5597.57	Large Cap
Dena Bank	Banking	PSU Bank	3216.14	Mid Cap
IDBI Bank Ltd.	Banking	PSU Bank	11396.11	Large Cap
Indian Bank	Banking	PSU Bank	10073.27	Large Cap
Indian Overseas Bank	Banking	PSU Bank	7405.91	Large Cap
Jammu & Kashmir Bank Ltd.	Banking	PSU Bank	7269.25	Large Cap
Oriental Bank of Commerce	Banking	PSU Bank	10151.38	Large Cap
Punjab & Sind Bank	Banking	PSU Bank	2460.53	Small Cap
Punjab National Bank	Banking	PSU Bank	39710.02	Large Cap
State Bank of Bikaner & Jaipur	Banking	PSU Bank	4263.00	Mid Cap
State Bank of India	Banking	PSU Bank	229496.57	Mega Cap

BSE 500 INDICES STOCK CLASSIFICATION - COMPANY, SECTOR, INDUSTRY & MARKET CAPITALIZATION (as on December 2014)				
COMPANY	SECTOR	INDUSTRY	Full Market Cap (in crore)	Market Cap Category
State Bank of Mysore	Banking	PSU Bank	2621.53	Mid Cap
State Bank of Travancore	Banking	PSU Bank	2958.82	Mid Cap
Syndicate Bank	Banking	PSU Bank	7950.96	Large Cap
UCO Bank	Banking	PSU Bank	8305.39	Large Cap
Union Bank of India	Banking	PSU Bank	15036.17	Large Cap
United Bank Of India	Banking	PSU Bank	2877.37	Mid Cap
Vijaya Bank	Banking	PSU Bank	4085.11	Mid Cap
Axis Bank Ltd.	Banking	Private Bank	116740.61	Mega Cap
City Union Bank Ltd.	Banking	Private Bank	5517.37	Large Cap
DCB Bank Ltd.	Banking	Private Bank	3437.03	Mid Cap
Dhanlaxmi Bank Ltd.	Banking	Private Bank	708.88	Micro Cap
Federal Bank Ltd.	Banking	Private Bank	12764.39	Large Cap
HDFC Bank Ltd.	Banking	Private Bank	230016.34	Mega Cap
ICICI Bank Ltd.	Banking	Private Bank	202321.01	Mega Cap
Indusind Bank Ltd.	Banking	Private Bank	41457.15	Large Cap
ING Vysya Bank Ltd.	Banking	Private Bank	16364.37	Large Cap
Karnataka Bank Ltd.	Banking	Private Bank	2709.75	Mid Cap
Kotak Mahindra Bank Ltd.	Banking	Private Bank	95938.15	Mega Cap
Lakshmi Vilas Bank Ltd.	Banking	Private Bank	1486.01	Small Cap
South Indian Bank Ltd.	Banking	Private Bank	3773.65	Mid Cap
Yes Bank Ltd.	Banking	Private Bank	30985.4	Large Cap
ALSTOM India Ltd.	Capital Goods	Heavy Electrical Equipments	4114.66	Mid Cap
Alstom T&D India Ltd.	Capital Goods	Electrical Utilities	11975.3	Large Cap
BEML Ltd	Capital Goods	Machinery manf.	2916.36	Mid Cap
Bharat Electronics Ltd.	Capital Goods	Electronic Equipts.	21832.00	Large Cap
Bharat Heavy Electricals Ltd.	Capital Goods	Electrical Machinery	62291.42	Mega Cap
Crompton Greaves Ltd.	Capital Goods	Electrical Machinery	11540.84	Large Cap
Cummins India Ltd.	Capital Goods	Electrical Machinery	24145.51	Large Cap
Elgi Equipments Ltd.	Capital Goods	Pumps & Compressors	2336.41	Small Cap
Greaves Cotton Ltd.	Capital Goods	Electronic Equipts.	3426.22	Mid Cap
Lakshmi Machine Works Ltd.	Capital Goods	Textile Machinery	4323.92	Mid Cap
Mahindra CIE Automotive Ltd.	Capital Goods	Industrial Machinery	1933.64	Small Cap
Praj Industries Ltd.	Capital Goods	Industrial Machinery	1063.9	Small Cap
Siemens Ltd.	Capital Goods	Switching Equipment	31028.73	Large Cap
SKF India Ltd.	Capital Goods	Industrial goods	7014.22	Large Cap
Thermax Ltd.	Capital Goods	Industrial Machinery	12695.51	Large Cap
Aarti Industries Ltd.	Chemicals	Organic Chemicals	2350.78	Small Cap
Akzo Nobel India Ltd.	Chemicals	Paints & Varnishes	6323.41	Large Cap
Asian Paints Ltd.	Chemicals	Paints & Varnishes	72640.05	Mega Cap
Astral Poly Technik Ltd.	Chemicals	Plastic Products	4609.14	Mid Cap
Atul Ltd.	Chemicals	Dyes & Pigments	3998.99	Mid Cap
BASF India Ltd.	Chemicals	Misc.Chem.	5242.76	Large Cap
Bayer CropScience Ltd.	Chemicals	Pesticides	11324.79	Large Cap
Berger Paints India Ltd.	Chemicals	Paints & Varnishes	14045.94	Large Cap
Chambal Fertilisers & Chemicals Ltd.	Chemicals	Fertilizers & Chemicals	2493.09	Mid Cap
Clariant Chemicals (India) Ltd.	Chemicals	Dyes & Pigments	2295.36	Mid Cap
Coromandel International Ltd.	Chemicals	Other Fertilisers	8692.22	Large Cap

BSE 500 INDICES STOCK CLASSIFICATION - COMPANY, SECTOR, INDUSTRY & MARKET CAPITALIZATION (as on December 2014)				
COMPANY	SECTOR	INDUSTRY	Full Market Cap (in crore)	Market Cap Category
Deepak Fertilisers & Petrochem. Corpn. Ltd.	Chemicals	Inorganic Chem.	1237.07	Small Cap
Finolex Industries Ltd.	Chemicals	Plastic tubes & pipes	3230.2	Mid Cap
Gujarat Alkalies & Chemicals Ltd.	Chemicals	Caustic Soda	1260.91	Small Cap
Gujarat Fluorochemicals Ltd.	Chemicals	Organic Chemicals	8442.52	Large Cap
Gujarat Narmada Valley Fert. & Chem. Ltd.	Chemicals	Fertilizers & Chemicals	1265.89	Small Cap
Gujarat State Fertilizers & Chemicals Ltd.	Chemicals	Fertilizers & Chemicals	4094.36	Mid Cap
Kansai Nerolac Paints Ltd.	Chemicals	Paints & Varnishes	10654.17	Large Cap
Linde India Ltd.	Chemicals	Industrial Gases	3708.16	Mid Cap
Monsanto India Ltd.	Chemicals	Pesticides	4781.61	Mid Cap
PI Industries Ltd.	Chemicals	Pesticides	6831.54	Large Cap
Pidilite Industries Ltd.	Chemicals	Thermoplastics	26737.93	Large Cap
Rashtriya Chemicals & Fertilizers Ltd.	Chemicals	Fertilizers & Chemicals	3737.69	Mid Cap
Solar Industries India Ltd.	Chemicals	Explosives	4913.25	Mid Cap
Supreme Industries Ltd.	Chemicals	Other Plastic Products.	7751.81	Large Cap
Tata Chemicals Ltd.	Chemicals	Soda Ash	10902.29	Large Cap
UFLEX Ltd.	Chemicals	Plastic Packaging goods	1101.59	Small Cap
UPL Ltd.	Chemicals	Inorganic Chem.	14411.82	Large Cap
ACC Ltd.	Construction	Cement	26309.7	Large Cap
Ambuja Cements Ltd.	Construction	Cement	35640.52	Large Cap
Anant Raj Ltd.	Construction	Real Estate	1341.21	Small Cap
Asahi India Glass Ltd.	Construction	Glass & Glassware	2816.2	Mid Cap
Birla Corporation Ltd.	Construction	Cement	3432.9	Mid Cap
CCL International Ltd.	Construction	Cement	3986.3	Mid Cap
Century Plyboards (India) Ltd.	Construction	Wood	3385.92	Mid Cap
Cera Sanitaryware Ltd.	Construction	Ceramic tiles	2174.17	Small Cap
Dalmia Bharat Ltd.	Construction	Cement	3555.69	Mid Cap
DB Realty Ltd.	Construction	Real Estate	1421.85	Small Cap
DLF Ltd.	Construction	Real Estate	24207.48	Large Cap
GMR Infrastructure Ltd	Construction	Infrastructure	7414.12	Large Cap
Godrej Properties Ltd.	Construction	Real Estate	4975.74	Mid Cap
Heidelberg Cement India Ltd.	Construction	Cement	1855.96	Small Cap
Hindustan Construction Co. Ltd.	Construction	Construction	1876.12	Small Cap
HDIL	Construction	Real Estate	2884.84	Mid Cap
HSIL Ltd.	Construction	Ceramic tiles	2342.67	Small Cap
India Cements Ltd.	Construction	Cement	2632.52	Mid Cap
Indiabulls Real Estate Ltd.	Construction	Real Estate	2913.22	Mid Cap
IRB Infrastructure Developers Ltd.	Construction	Construction	8403.83	Large Cap
IVRCL Ltd.	Construction	Infrastructure	631.79	Micro Cap
Jai Prakash Associates Ltd.	Construction	Infrastructure (cement etc.)	6336.55	Large Cap
Jain Irrigation Systems Ltd.	Construction	Plastic tubes & pipes	3024.29	Mid Cap
Jaypee Infratech Ltd	Construction	Infrastructure	2916.76	Mid Cap
JK Cement Ltd	Construction	Cement	4422.55	Mid Cap
JK Lakshmi Cement Ltd.	Construction	Cement	4833.30	Mid Cap
Kajaria Ceramics Ltd.	Construction	Ceramic tiles	4498.74	Mid Cap
Kolte Patil Developers Ltd.	Construction	Real Estate	1392.74	Small Cap
Lanco Infratech Ltd.	Construction	Infrastructure	1408.57	Small Cap
Mahindra Lifespace Developers Ltd.	Construction	Real Estate	1914.39	Small Cap

BSE 500 INDICES STOCK CLASSIFICATION - COMPANY, SECTOR, INDUSTRY & MARKET CAPITALIZATION (as on December 2014)				
COMPANY	SECTOR	INDUSTRY	Full Market Cap (in crore)	Market Cap Category
National Buildings Construction Corp. Ltd.	Construction	Real Estate	9387.00	Large Cap
NCC Ltd.	Construction	Construction	4400.20	Mid Cap
Nesco Ltd.	Construction	Real Estate	2391.69	Small Cap
Nitin Fire Protection Industries Ltd.	Construction	Diversified	914.8	Micro Cap
Oberoi Realty Ltd.	Construction	Real Estate	9082.21	Large Cap
Omaxe Ltd.	Construction	Real Estate	2266.14	Small Cap
Orient Cement Ltd.	Construction	Cement & Asbestos products	3043.33	Mid Cap
Phoenix Mills Ltd.	Construction	Real Estate	5349.18	Large Cap
Prestige Estates Projects Ltd.	Construction	Real Estate	9082.5	Large Cap
Prism Cement Ltd.	Construction	Cement	3976.52	Mid Cap
Punj Lloyd Ltd.	Construction	Infrastructure	1220.45	Small Cap
Puravankara Projects Ltd.	Construction	Real Estate	1933.96	Small Cap
Rain Industries Ltd.	Construction	Cement & Asbestos prod.	1520.28	Small Cap
Reliance Industrial Infrastructure Ltd.	Construction	Infrastructure	699.05	Micro Cap
Reliance Infrastructure Ltd.	Construction	Electricity Distribn.	13370.41	Large Cap
Sadbhav Engineering Ltd.	Construction	Construction	4203.75	Mid Cap
Shree Cement Ltd.	Construction	Cement	32447.22	Large Cap
Sintex Industries Ltd.	Construction	Diversified	3498.07	Mid Cap
Sobha Ltd.	Construction	Real Estate	4611.94	Mid Cap
Sunteck Realty Ltd.	Construction	Real Estate	1798.00	Small Cap
The Ramco Cements Ltd.	Construction	Cement	8000.53	Large Cap
Ultratech Cement Ltd.	Construction	Cement	72528.94	Mega Cap
Unitech Ltd.	Construction	Real Estate	4369.22	Mid Cap
Bajaj Electricals Ltd.	Consumer Durable	Domestic Electrical Applns.	2203.58	Small Cap
Blue Star Ltd.	Consumer Durable	ACs & Refrigerators	2788.47	Mid Cap
Gitanjali Gems Ltd.	Consumer Durable	Gems & Jewellery	530.83	Micro Cap
Hawkins Cookers Ltd.	Consumer Durable	Domestic Electrical Applns.	1946.95	Small Cap
PC Jeweller Ltd.	Consumer Durable	Gems & Jewellery	3767.37	Mid Cap
Symphony Ltd.	Consumer Durable	ACs & Refrigerators	6481.87	Large Cap
Tribhovandas Bhimji Zaveri Ltd	Consumer Durable	Gems & Jewellery	984.12	Micro Cap
TTK Prestige Ltd.	Consumer Durable	Domestic Electrical Applns.	4080.48	Mid Cap
Vaibhav Global Ltd.	Consumer Durable	Gems & Jewellery	2104.62	Small Cap
V-Guard Industries Ltd.	Consumer Durable	Domestic Electrical Applns.	3283.96	Mid Cap
Videocon Industries Ltd.	Consumer Durable	Consumer Electronics	5408.20	Large Cap
Voltas Ltd.	Consumer Durable	ACs & Refrigerators	7807.23	Large Cap
Whirlpool Of India Ltd.	Consumer Durable	ACs & Refrigerators	8079.83	Large Cap
United Breweries Ltd.	Distilleries	Liquors	21900.68	Large Cap
United Spirits Ltd.	Distilleries	Liquors	40252.15	Large Cap
Aditya Birla Nuvo Ltd.	Diversified	Diversified (textiles)	21829.96	Large Cap
Century Textiles & Inds. Ltd.	Diversified	Diversified (textiles)	4828.61	Mid Cap
DCM Shriram Ltd.	Diversified	Diversified (agri & chemicals)	2652.26	Mid Cap
Grasim Industries Ltd.	Diversified	Diversified (textiles & cement)	31415.51	Large Cap
Kesoram Industries Ltd.	Diversified	Diversified (cement, textiles)	1065.85	Small Cap
Nava Bharat Ventures Ltd.	Diversified	Diversified (power, mining, agri)	1757.18	Small Cap
Rallis India Ltd.	Diversified	Diversified (agri products)	4078.01	Mid Cap
ABB Ltd.	Engineering	Switching Equipment	25917.45	Large Cap
Engineers India Ltd.	Engineering	Consulting	7678.79	Large Cap

BSE 500 INDICES STOCK CLASSIFICATION - COMPANY, SECTOR, INDUSTRY & MARKET CAPITALIZATION (as on December 2014)				
COMPANY	SECTOR	INDUSTRY	Full Market Cap (in crore)	Market Cap Category
FAG Bearings India Ltd.	Engineering	Ball Bearings	5848.03	Large Cap
Finolex Cables Ltd.	Engineering	Wires & cables	3946.6	Mid Cap
Graphite India Ltd.	Engineering	Welding machinery	1696.84	Small Cap
Havells India Ltd.	Engineering	Switching Equipment	16929.87	Large Cap
Honeywell Automation India Ltd.	Engineering	Electronic Equipts.	6105.91	Large Cap
Ingersoll Rand India Ltd.	Engineering	Pumps & Compressors	2704.75	Mid Cap
Larsen & Toubro Ltd.	Engineering	Diversified (engg. & infra)	138612.17	Mega Cap
Schneider Electric Infrastructure Ltd.	Engineering	Electronic Components	3593.73	Mid Cap
Texmaco Rail & Engineering Ltd.	Engineering	Other Machinery	2749.74	Mid Cap
Timken India Ltd.	Engineering	Industrial Machinery	3495.88	Mid Cap
Triveni Turbine Ltd.	Engineering	Industrial Machinery	3486.16	Mid Cap
VA Tech Wabag Ltd	Engineering	Other Machinery	4112.71	Mid Cap
Bajaj Finance Ltd.	Financial Services	Lending	17427.18	Large Cap
Bajaj Finserv Ltd.	Financial Services	Lending & ancillary	21073.74	Large Cap
Bajaj Holdings & Investment Ltd.	Financial Services	Invest.Services	15540.47	Large Cap
Capital First Ltd.	Financial Services	Invest.Services	2952.39	Mid Cap
Cholamandalam Invt. & Finance Co. Ltd.	Financial Services	Lending	6987.1	Large Cap
Credit Analysis & Research Ltd (CARE)	Financial Services	Credit Ratings & Information	4116.72	Mid Cap
Cressanda Solutions Ltd.	Financial Services	Misc. Fin.services	1476.9	Small Cap
Crisil Ltd.	Financial Services	Credit Ratings & Information	13775.12	Large Cap
Dewan Housing Finance Corpn. Ltd.	Financial Services	Housing Finance	5091.99	Large Cap
Dhanleela Invts. & Trading Co. Ltd.	Financial Services	Misc. Fin.services	686.21	Micro Cap
Edelweiss Financial Services Ltd.	Financial Services	Invest.Services	3947.97	Mid Cap
Future Consumer Enterprise Ltd.	Financial Services	Invest.Services	2022.09	Small Cap
GIC Housing Finance Ltd.	Financial Services	Housing Finance	1049.29	Small Cap
Gold Line International Finvest Ltd.	Financial Services	Invest.Services	2586.59	Mid Cap
Greencrest Financial Services Ltd.	Financial Services	Misc. commercial services	2266.15	Small Cap
Gruh Finance Ltd.	Financial Services	Housing Finance	9720.34	Large Cap
HDFC Ltd.	Financial Services	Housing Finance	176652.42	Mega Cap
ICRA Ltd.	Financial Services	Credit Ratings & Information	2943.4	Mid Cap
IDFC Ltd.	Financial Services	Infrastructure lending	25022.06	Large Cap
IFCI Ltd.	Financial Services	Development financial insti.	6265.88	Large Cap
IIFL Holdings Ltd.	Financial Services	Invest.Services	5000.00	Large Cap
Indiabulls Housing Finance Ltd.	Financial Services	Housing Finance	15912.67	Large Cap
JM Financial Ltd.	Financial Services	Misc. Fin.services	3579.79	Mid Cap
JSW Holdings Ltd.	Financial Services	Invest.Services	1040.15	Small Cap
Kailash Auto Finance Ltd.	Financial Services	Hire Purchase	473.17	Micro Cap
L&T Finance Holdings Ltd.	Financial Services	Misc. Fin.services	11543.9	Large Cap
LIC Housing Finance Ltd.	Financial Services	Housing Finance	21140.33	Large Cap
Magma Fincorp Ltd.	Financial Services	Equipt.Leasing	1917.15	Small Cap
Mahindra & Mahindra Fin. Serv. Ltd.	Financial Services	Misc. Fin.services	17375.77	Large Cap
Manappuram Finance Ltd.	Financial Services	Hire Purchase	2771.78	Small Cap
Max India Ltd.	Financial Services	Invest.Services	10262.61	Large Cap
Motilal Oswal Financial Services Ltd	Financial Services	Misc. Fin.services	3534.52	Mid Cap
Multi Commodity Exchange India	Financial Services	Misc. Fin.services	4295.34	Mid Cap
Muthoot Finance Ltd.	Financial Services	Misc. Fin.services	7611.71	Large Cap
Pine Animation Ltd.	Financial Services	Hire Purchase	1979.16	Small Cap

BSE 500 INDICES STOCK CLASSIFICATION - COMPANY, SECTOR, INDUSTRY & MARKET CAPITALIZATION (as on December 2014)				
COMPANY	SECTOR	INDUSTRY	Full Market Cap (in crore)	Market Cap Category
PMC Fincorp Ltd.	Financial Services	Misc. Fin.services	2201.69	Small Cap
Power Finance Corpn. Ltd.	Financial Services	Small scale indl. lending	39442.82	Large Cap
PS IT Infrastructure & Services Ltd.	Financial Services	Invest.Services	4499.71	Mid Cap
PTC India Financial Services Ltd.	Financial Services	Misc. Fin.services	3541.13	Mid Cap
Reliance Capital Ltd.	Financial Services	Equipt.Leasing	12193.21	Large Cap
Religare Enterprises Ltd.	Financial Services	Invest.Services	6188.04	Large Cap
Repco Home Finance Ltd.	Financial Services	Housing Finance	3981.06	Mid Cap
Rural Electrification Corpn. Ltd.	Financial Services	Small scale indl. lending	32921.88	Large Cap
SE Investment Ltd.	Financial Services	Invt. Services	979.12	Micro Cap
Shriram City Union Finance Ltd.	Financial Services	Equipt.Leasing	12589.54	Large Cap
Shriram Transport Finance Co. Ltd.	Financial Services	Equipt.Leasing	24986.6	Large Cap
SKS Microfinance Ltd.	Financial Services	Misc. Fin.services	5010.79	Large Cap
SREI Infrastructure Finance Ltd.	Financial Services	Equipt.Leasing	2397.21	Small Cap
Standard Chartered PLC (UK)	Financial Services	Banking	2157.6	Small Cap
Sulabh Engineers & Services Ltd.	Financial Services	Hire Purchase	1662.36	Small Cap
Surabhi Chemicals & Investment Ltd.	Financial Services	Misc. Fin.services	2337.23	Small Cap
Tata Investment Corpn. Ltd.	Financial Services	Invest.Services	3093.6	Mid Cap
Tilak Finance Ltd.	Financial Services	Invest.Services	3385.45	Mid Cap
Westlife Development Ltd.	Financial Services	Hire Purchase	4565.69	Mid Cap
Advanta Ltd.	FMCG	Vegetable oils	3001.5	Mid Cap
Bajaj Corp Ltd.	FMCG	Cosmetics & Toiletries	5039.34	Large Cap
Bajaj Hindusthan Ltd.	FMCG	Sugar	1202.07	Small Cap
Balrampur Chini Mills Ltd.	FMCG	Sugar	1419.29	Small Cap
Britannia Industries Ltd.	FMCG	Bakery & Milling Prod.	21401.36	Large Cap
CCL Products (India) Ltd.	FMCG	Tea & Coffee	2203.61	Small Cap
Colgate-Palmolive (India) Ltd.	FMCG	Cosmetics & Toiletries	24227.8	Large Cap
Dabur India Ltd.	FMCG	Cosmetics & Toiletries	40162.65	Large Cap
EID-Parry (India) Ltd.	FMCG	Sugar	3489.93	Mid Cap
Emami Ltd.	FMCG	Personal Care	17934.98	Large Cap
Gillette India Ltd.	FMCG	Cosmetics & Toiletries	10603.07	Large Cap
Glaxosmithkline Consumer Healthcare Ltd.	FMCG	Dairy products	24376.44	Large Cap
Godfrey Phillips India Ltd.	FMCG	Tobacco Prod.	3027.61	Mid Cap
Godrej Consumer Products Ltd.	FMCG	Cosmetics & Toiletries	32495.28	Large Cap
Godrej Industries Ltd.	FMCG	Cosmetics & Toiletries	9718.14	Large Cap
Hatsun Agro Products Ltd.	FMCG	Dairy products	3399.33	Mid Cap
Hindustan Unilever Ltd.	FMCG	Cosmetics & Toiletries	164102.73	Mega Cap
ITC Ltd.	FMCG	Tobacco Prod.	295751.16	Mega Cap
Jyothy Laboratories Ltd.	FMCG	Cosmetics & Toiletries	4579.89	Mid Cap
KRBL Ltd.	FMCG	Packaged food	2318.59	Small Cap
Marico Ltd.	FMCG	Personal Care	21203.42	Large Cap
Mcleod Russel (India) Ltd.	FMCG	Tea & Coffee	2500.40	Mid Cap
Nestle India Ltd.	FMCG	Dairy products	59335.68	Mega Cap
Procter & Gamble	FMCG	Cosmetics & Toiletries	18887.44	Large Cap
Radico Khaitan Ltd.	FMCG	Liquors	1159.43	Small Cap
Rasoya Proteins Ltd.	FMCG	Soyabean Prod.	242.67	Micro Cap
Ruchi Soya Inds. Ltd.	FMCG	Soyabean Prod.	1234.35	Small Cap
Shree Renuka Sugars Ltd.	FMCG	Sugar	1435.01	Small Cap

BSE 500 INDICES STOCK CLASSIFICATION - COMPANY, SECTOR, INDUSTRY & MARKET CAPITALIZATION (as on December 2014)				
COMPANY	SECTOR	INDUSTRY	Full Market Cap (in crore)	Market Cap Category
Tata Coffee Ltd.	FMCG	Tea & Coffee	1760.59	Small Cap
Tata Global Beverages Ltd.	FMCG	Tea & Coffee	9180.13	Large Cap
VST Industries Ltd.	FMCG	Tobacco Prod.	2946.63	Mid Cap
Zydus Wellness Ltd.	FMCG	Packaged food	3155.07	Mid Cap
Apollo Hospitals Enterprise Ltd.	Healthcare	Hospitals	15748.97	Large Cap
Fortis Healthcare (India) Ltd	Healthcare	Hospitals	4940.27	Mid Cap
Opto Circuits (India) Ltd.	Healthcare	healthcare Components	617.91	Micro Cap
CMC Ltd.	IT	Computer Hardware	5833.2	Large Cap
Cyient Limited	IT	Computer Software	5787.03	Large Cap
Financial Technologies (India) Ltd.	IT	Computer Software	951.06	Micro Cap
Geometric Ltd.	IT	Computer Software	810.25	Micro Cap
HCL Infosystems Ltd.	IT	Computer Hardware	1167.94	Small Cap
HCL Technologies Ltd.	IT	Computer Software	110732.29	Mega Cap
Hexaware Technologies Ltd.	IT	Computer Software	5892.68	Mid Cap
Infosys Ltd.	IT	Computer Software	225077.61	Mega Cap
MindTree Ltd.	IT	Computer Software	10240.61	Large Cap
Mphasis Ltd.	IT	Computer Software	7663.64	Large Cap
Oracle Financial Serv. Software Ltd.	IT	Computer Software	28664.16	Large Cap
Persistent Systems Ltd.	IT	Computer Software	6569.2	Large Cap
Rolta India Ltd.	IT	Computer Hardware	1499.55	Small Cap
Sonata Software Ltd.	IT	Computer Software	1321.85	Small Cap
Tata Consultancy Services Ltd.	IT	Computer Software	494520.05	Mega Cap
Tech Mahindra Ltd.	IT	Computer Software	62084.66	Mega Cap
Vakrangee Ltd.	IT	Computer Software	6182.76	Large Cap
Wipro Ltd.	IT	Computer Software	135869.09	Mega Cap
Accelya Kale Solutions Ltd.	ITES	Computer Software	1462.92	Small Cap
eClerx Services Ltd	ITES	Technology driven serv.	3969.14	Mid Cap
Firstsource Solutions Ltd.	ITES	Technology driven serv.	2251.50	Small Cap
KPIT Technologies Ltd.	ITES	Technology driven serv.	3917.68	Mid Cap
NIIT Technologies Ltd.	ITES	Technology driven serv.	2138.18	Small Cap
Polaris Consulting & Services Ltd.	ITES	Technology driven serv.	1693.01	Small Cap
Redington India Ltd.	ITES	Technology driven serv.	5475.39	Large Cap
Tata Elxsi Ltd.	ITES	Technology driven serv.	1828.44	Small Cap
Ybrant Digital Ltd.	ITES	Technology driven serv.	2319.34	Small Cap
Zensar Technologies Ltd.	ITES	Technology driven serv.	2669.95	Mid Cap
DB Corporation Ltd.	Media & Entertainment	Publishing	6990.81	Large Cap
Den Networks Ltd.	Media & Entertainment	Recreational Services	2391.44	Small Cap
Entertainment Network India Ltd.	Media & Entertainment	Recreational Services	2396.15	Small Cap
Eros International Media Ltd.	Media & Entertainment	Recreational Services	3440.26	Mid Cap
HT Media Ltd.	Media & Entertainment	Recreational Services	2869.79	Mid Cap
INOX Leisure Ltd.	Media & Entertainment	Recreational Services	1688.49	Small Cap
Jagran Prakashan Ltd.	Media & Entertainment	Recreational Services	4325.04	Mid Cap
Navneet Education Ltd.	Media & Entertainment	Books & Newspapers	2595.35	Mid Cap
Network 18 Media & Invts. Ltd.	Media & Entertainment	Recreational Services	6793.82	Large Cap
PVR Ltd.	Media & Entertainment	Recreational Services	2881.22	Mid Cap
Siti Cable Network Ltd.	Media & Entertainment	Recreational Services	2097.54	Small Cap
Sun TV Network Ltd.	Media & Entertainment	Recreational Services	15235.31	Large Cap

BSE 500 INDICES STOCK CLASSIFICATION - COMPANY, SECTOR, INDUSTRY & MARKET CAPITALIZATION (as on December 2014)				
COMPANY	SECTOR	INDUSTRY	Full Market Cap (in crore)	Market Cap Category
TV Today Network Ltd.	Media & Entertainment	Recreational Services	1263.87	Small Cap
TV18 Broadcast Ltd.	Media & Entertainment	Recreational Services	5253.86	Large Cap
Zee Entertainment Enterprises Ltd.	Media & Entertainment	Recreational Services	36444.23	Large Cap
Ahmednagar Forgings Ltd.	Metal	Castings & Forgings	1228.00	Small Cap
AIA Engineering Ltd.	Metal	Castings & Forgings	10001.73	Large Cap
Balmer Lawrie & Co. Ltd.	Metal	Metal Tanks & Fabrications	1727.42	Small Cap
Carborundum Universal Ltd.	Metal	Abrasives	3259.91	Mid Cap
Ess Dee Aluminium Ltd.	Metal	Aluminium Prod.	1119.75	Small Cap
Grindwell Norton Ltd.	Metal	Abrasives	3240.77	Mid Cap
Hindalco Industries Ltd.	Metal	Aluminium	32440.58	Large Cap
Hindustan Copper Ltd.	Metal	Other Non-Ferrous Metal	6536.67	Large Cap
Hindustan Zinc Ltd.	Metal	Other Non-Ferrous Metal	70499.45	Mega Cap
Jindal Saw Ltd.	Metal	Steel Tubes & Pipes	2539.88	Mid Cap
Maharashtra Seamless Ltd.	Metal	Steel Tubes & Pipes	1637.47	Small Cap
National Aluminium Co. Ltd.	Metal	Aluminium	14020.18	Large Cap
Sesa Sterlite Ltd.	Metal	Minerals	63829.76	Mega Cap
Tata Sponge Iron Ltd.	Metal	Sponge Iron	1069.53	Small Cap
Usha Martin Ltd.	Metal	Other Metal prod.	804.52	Micro Cap
Gujarat Mineral Devp. Corpn. Ltd.	Mining	Coal & Lignite	3938.43	Mid Cap
MMTC Ltd.	Mining	Trading	5660.00	Large Cap
Moil Ltd.	Mining	Minerals	5016.48	Large Cap
NMDC Ltd.	Mining	Minerals	56913.50	Mega Cap
Aban Offshore Ltd.	Oil, Gas & Exploration	Offshore Drilling	2790.38	Mid Cap
Bharat Petroleum Corpn. Ltd.	Oil, Gas & Exploration	Crude Oil & Natural Gas	46732.93	Large Cap
Cairn India Ltd.	Oil, Gas & Exploration	Crude Oil & Natural Gas	44919.08	Large Cap
Chennai Petroleum Corpn. Ltd.	Oil, Gas & Exploration	Crude Oil & Natural Gas	1054.29	Small Cap
Coal India Ltd.	Oil, Gas & Exploration	Coal & Lignite	243969.57	Mega Cap
Essar Oil Ltd.	Oil, Gas & Exploration	Crude Oil & Natural Gas	15546.07	Large Cap
GAIL (India) Ltd.	Oil, Gas & Exploration	Crude Oil & Natural Gas	56111.10	Large Cap
Gujarat Gas Co. Ltd.	Oil, Gas & Exploration	Storage & Distribn.	10124.06	Large Cap
Gujarat State Petronet Ltd.	Oil, Gas & Exploration	Storage & Distribn.	6379.58	Large Cap
Hindustan Petroleum Corpn. Ltd.	Oil, Gas & Exploration	Crude Oil & Natural Gas	18421.32	Large Cap
Indian Oil Corpn. Ltd.	Oil, Gas & Exploration	Crude Oil & Natural Gas	80547.32	Mega Cap
Indraprastha Gas Ltd.	Oil, Gas & Exploration	Storage & Distribn.	6455.41	Large Cap
Mangalore Refinery & Petrochemicals Ltd.	Oil, Gas & Exploration	Crude Oil & Natural Gas	8263.50	Large Cap
Oil & Natural Gas Corpn. Ltd.	Oil, Gas & Exploration	Crude Oil & Natural Gas	296490.51	Mega Cap
Oil India Ltd.	Oil, Gas & Exploration	Crude Oil & Natural Gas	33982.22	Large Cap
Reliance Industries Ltd.	Oil, Gas & Exploration	Crude Oil & Natural Gas	290185.77	Mega Cap
Selan Exploration Technology Ltd.	Oil, Gas & Exploration	Offshore Drilling	578.43	Micro Cap
Petronet LNG Ltd.	Oil, Gas & Exploration	Crude Oil & Natural Gas	15603.75	Large Cap
Ballarpur Industries Ltd.	Paper Products	Paper Products	1009.51	Small Cap
International Paper APPM Ltd.	Paper Products	Paper Products	944.94	Micro Cap
Tamil Nadu Newsprint & Papers Ltd.	Paper Products	Paper Products	892.82	Micro Cap
Abbott India Ltd.	Pharmaceuticals	Drugs & Pharma	7883.17	Large Cap
Ajanta Pharma Ltd.	Pharmaceuticals	Drugs & Pharma	8305.56	Large Cap
Alembic Pharmaceuticals Ltd.	Pharmaceuticals	Drugs & Pharma	8251.34	Large Cap
Astrazeneca Pharma India Ltd.	Pharmaceuticals	Drugs & Pharma	2008.12	Small Cap

BSE 500 INDICES STOCK CLASSIFICATION - COMPANY, SECTOR, INDUSTRY & MARKET CAPITALIZATION (as on December 2014)				
COMPANY	SECTOR	INDUSTRY	Full Market Cap (in crore)	Market Cap Category
Aurobindo Pharma Ltd.	Pharmaceuticals	Drugs & Pharma	32333.64	Large Cap
Biocon Ltd.	Pharmaceuticals	Drugs & Pharma	8349.00	Large Cap
Cadila Healthcare Ltd.	Pharmaceuticals	Drugs & Pharma	32102.52	Large Cap
Cipla Ltd.	Pharmaceuticals	Drugs & Pharma	50001.93	Mega Cap
Dishman Pharma & Chemicals Ltd.	Pharmaceuticals	Drugs & Pharma	978.86	Micro Cap
Divi's Laboratories Ltd.	Pharmaceuticals	Drugs & Pharma	22651.77	Large Cap
Dr. Reddy's Laboratories Ltd.	Pharmaceuticals	Drugs & Pharma	53502.54	Mega Cap
FDC Ltd.	Pharmaceuticals	Drugs & Pharma	2834.66	Mid Cap
Glaxosmithkline Pharmaceuticals Ltd.	Pharmaceuticals	Drugs & Pharma	26676.79	Large Cap
Glenmark Pharmaceuticals Ltd.	Pharmaceuticals	Drugs & Pharma	21222.57	Large Cap
Granules India Ltd.	Pharmaceuticals	Drugs & Pharma	1618.8	Small Cap
Indoco Remedies Ltd.	Pharmaceuticals	Drugs & Pharma	2727.19	Mid Cap
Ipca Laboratories Ltd.	Pharmaceuticals	Drugs & Pharma	9336.84	Large Cap
JB Chemicals & Pharmaceuticals Ltd.	Pharmaceuticals	Drugs & Pharma	1683.44	Small Cap
Jubilant Life Sciences Ltd	Pharmaceuticals	Drugs & Pharma	1889.07	Small Cap
Kappac Pharma Ltd.	Pharmaceuticals	Drugs & Pharma	463.86	Micro Cap
Lupin Ltd.	Pharmaceuticals	Drugs & Pharma	64315.9	Mega Cap
Marksans Pharma Ltd.	Pharmaceuticals	Drugs & Pharma	2383.13	Small Cap
Natco Pharma Ltd.	Pharmaceuticals	Drugs & Pharma	4536.89	Mid Cap
Novartis India Ltd.	Pharmaceuticals	Drugs & Pharma	2078.09	Small Cap
Orchid Chemicals & Pharma Ltd.	Pharmaceuticals	Drugs & Pharma	561.88	Micro Cap
Pfizer Ltd.	Pharmaceuticals	Drugs & Pharma	6061.99	Large Cap
Piramal Enterprises Ltd.	Pharmaceuticals	Drugs & Pharma	13987.96	Large Cap
Ranbaxy Laboratories Ltd.	Pharmaceuticals	Drugs & Pharma	26555.43	Large Cap
Sanofi India Ltd.	Pharmaceuticals	Drugs & Pharma	8181.97	Large Cap
Shasun Pharmaceuticals Ltd.	Pharmaceuticals	Drugs & Pharma	1643.79	Small Cap
Strides Arcolab Ltd.	Pharmaceuticals	Drugs & Pharma	5451.15	Large Cap
Sun Pharma Advanced Research Co. Ltd.	Pharmaceuticals	Drugs & Pharma	4310.39	Mid Cap
Sun Pharmaceutical Inds. Ltd.	Pharmaceuticals	Drugs & Pharma	169887.22	Mega Cap
Suven Life Sciences Ltd.	Pharmaceuticals	Drugs & Pharma	2641.75	Mid Cap
Torrent Pharmaceuticals Ltd.	Pharmaceuticals	Drugs & Pharma	18639.88	Large Cap
Unichem Laboratories Ltd.	Pharmaceuticals	Drugs & Pharma	2207.52	Small Cap
Wockhardt Ltd.	Pharmaceuticals	Drugs & Pharma	11111.88	Large Cap
Adani Power Ltd.	Power	Power Projects	12363.62	Large Cap
BF Utilities Ltd.	Power	Electricity Generation	2434.46	Small Cap
BGR Energy Systems Ltd.	Power	Electrical Machinery	1109.48	Small Cap
CESC Ltd.	Power	Electricity Generation	8824.99	Large Cap
GVK Power & Infrastructure Ltd.	Power	Electricity Generation	1430.76	Small Cap
Jaiprakash Power Ventures Limited	Power	Electricity Generation	3552.05	Mid Cap
JSW Energy Ltd.	Power	Power Projects	16326.75	Large Cap
Kalpataru Power Transmission Ltd.	Power	Power Projects	3356.95	Mid Cap
KEC International Ltd.	Power	Power Projects	2297.08	Small Cap
KSK Energy Ventures Ltd.	Power	Power Projects	2814.83	Mid Cap
National Thermal Power Corp. Ltd.	Power	Electricity Generation	115395.27	Mega Cap
Neyveli Lignite Corpn. Ltd.	Power	Electricity Generation	13472.01	Large Cap
NHPC Ltd.	Power	Electricity Generation	20868.21	Large Cap
Power Grid Corpn. Of India Ltd.	Power	Electricity Distribn.	71620.46	Mega Cap

BSE 500 INDICES STOCK CLASSIFICATION - COMPANY, SECTOR, INDUSTRY & MARKET CAPITALIZATION (as on December 2014)				
COMPANY	SECTOR	INDUSTRY	Full Market Cap (in crore)	Market Cap Category
PTC India Ltd.	Power	Electricity Distribn.	2763.24	Mid Cap
RattanIndia Power Ltd.	Power	Power Projects	2843.67	Mid Cap
Reliance Power Ltd.	Power	Electricity Generation	17363.73	Large Cap
SJVN Ltd.	Power	Electricity Generation	9886.54	Large Cap
Suzlon Energy Ltd.	Power	Electrical Machinery	4195.65	Mid Cap
Swan Energy Ltd.	Power	Real Estate	1220.91	Small Cap
Tata Power Co. Ltd.	Power	Electricity Generation	22015.65	Large Cap
Torrent Power Ltd.	Power	Electricity Distribn.	7637.13	Large Cap
Bata India Ltd.	Retail	Footwear	8394.13	Large Cap
Future Lifestyle Fashion Ltd.	Retail	Clothing & Accessories	1644.15	Small Cap
Future Retail Ltd.	Retail	Clothing & Accessories	3969.38	Mid Cap
Shopper's Stop Ltd	Retail	Clothing & Accessories	4187.65	Mid Cap
Titan Company Ltd.	Retail	Gems & Jewellery	33181.01	Large Cap
Trent Ltd.	Retail	Personal Accessories	4935.22	Mid Cap
VIP Industries Ltd.	Retail	Plastic Packaging goods	1586.29	Small Cap
3M India Ltd.	Services	Trading	7294.81	Large Cap
ABG Shipyard Ltd	Services	Shipping	1164.13	Small Cap
Adani Enterprises Ltd.	Services	Trading	50442.79	Mega Cap
Adani Ports	Services	Shipping	60611.11	Mega Cap
Allcargo Logistics Ltd.	Services	Logistics & Transportation	3894.88	Mid Cap
Blue Dart Express Ltd.	Services	Logistics & Transportation	14752.13	Large Cap
Container Corpn. Of India Ltd.	Services	Logistics & Transportation	25817.51	Large Cap
Cox & Kings Ltd.	Services	Tourism	4859.34	Mid Cap
Delta Corp Ltd.	Services	Miscellaneous commercial serv	2048.88	Small Cap
Dish TV India Ltd.	Services	Cable television	6965.15	Large Cap
EIH Ltd.	Services	Hotels & Restaurants	6758.81	Large Cap
Essar Ports Ltd.	Services	Shipping	4358.04	Mid Cap
Gateway Distriparks Ltd.	Services	Logistics & Transportation	3798.41	Mid Cap
Gati Ltd.	Services	Logistics & Transportation	2189.89	Small Cap
Great Eastern Shipping Company Ltd.	Services	Shipping	5325.45	Large Cap
Gujarat Pipavav Port Ltd	Services	Shipping	9209.53	Large Cap
Hinduja Global Solutions Ltd.	Services	Misc.Other Services	1303.18	Small Cap
IL&FS Transportation Networks Ltd.	Services	Logistics & Transportation	4585.29	Mid Cap
Indian Hotels Co. Ltd.	Services	Hotels & Restaurants	9855.21	Large Cap
Info Edge (India) Ltd.	Services	Job portal & ancillary services	10108.38	Large Cap
Jubilant FoodWorks Ltd.	Services	Hotels & Restaurants	8803.24	Large Cap
Just Dial Ltd.	Services	ITES	9444.34	Large Cap
Mahindra Holidays & Resorts India Ltd	Services	Tourism	2232.84	Small Cap
Pipavav Defence and Offshore Engg. Co. Ltd.	Services	Shipping	2952.19	Mid Cap
Rajesh Exports Ltd.	Services	Gems & Jewellery	4114.45	Mid Cap
Risa International Ltd.	Services	Clothing & Accessories	5084.07	Large Cap
Shipping Corpn. Of India Ltd.	Services	Shipping	2706.29	Mid Cap
State Trading Corpn. Of India Ltd.	Services	Trading (export/import support)	1095.6	Small Cap
Sunrise Asian Ltd.	Services	Trading (textile, chemicals)	2019.45	Small Cap
The Byke Hospitality Ltd.	Services	Hotels & Restaurants	601.47	Micro Cap
Thomas Cook (India) Ltd.	Services	Tourism	4113.21	Mid Cap
Tree House Education & Accessories Ltd.	Services	Education	1846.86	Small Cap

BSE 500 INDICES STOCK CLASSIFICATION - COMPANY, SECTOR, INDUSTRY & MARKET CAPITALIZATION (as on December 2014)				
COMPANY	SECTOR	INDUSTRY	Full Market Cap (in crore)	Market Cap Category
Trinity Tradelink Ltd.	Services	Misc. Manuf.Articles	406.96	Micro Cap
Wonderla Holidays Ltd	Services	Recreational Services	1643.04	Small Cap
Bhushan Steel Ltd.	Steel	Finished Steel	1995.59	Small Cap
Jai Corp Ltd.	Steel	Finished Steel	1292.87	Small Cap
Jindal Steel & Power Ltd.	Steel	Sponge Iron	14116.97	Large Cap
JSW Steel Ltd.	Steel	Finished Steel	25872.72	Large Cap
Steel Authority Of India Ltd.	Steel	Finished Steel	34242.05	Large Cap
Tata Steel Ltd.	Steel	Finished Steel	39266.24	Large Cap
Welspun Corp Ltd.	Steel	Steel Tubes & Pipes	1767.01	Small Cap
Astra Microwave Products Ltd.	Telecom	Communication Equipt.	924.63	Micro Cap
Bharti Airtel Ltd.	Telecom	Telecom.Services	140548.59	Mega Cap
Bharti Infratel Ltd.	Telecom	Telecom.Services	61357.9	Mega Cap
Hathway Cable & Datacom Ltd.	Telecom	Telecom.Services	5748.68	Mega Cap
Himachal Futuristic Communications Ltd.	Telecom	Communication Equipt.	2249.47	Small Cap
Idea Cellular Ltd.	Telecom	Telecom.Services	54173.04	Mega Cap
Mahanagar Telephone Nigam Ltd.	Telecom	Telecom.Services	1713.6	Small Cap
Reliance Communications Ltd.	Telecom	Telecom.Services	19398.68	Large Cap
Sterlite Technologies Ltd.	Telecom	Communication Equipt.	2353.99	Small Cap
Tata Communications Ltd.	Telecom	Telecom.Services	12257.85	Large Cap
Tata Teleservices (Maharashtra) Ltd.	Telecom	Telecom.Services	1489.65	Small Cap
Alok Industries Ltd.	Textiles	Clothing	1393.85	Small Cap
Arvind Ltd.	Textiles	Clothing	7238.55	Large Cap
Bombay Dyeing & Mfg. Co. Ltd.	Textiles	Clothing	1355.9	Small Cap
Effingo Textiles & Trading Ltd.	Textiles	Misc.Textiles	687.25	Micro Cap
Kitex Garments Ltd.	Textiles	Readymade Garments	2389.72	Small Cap
Page Industries Ltd.	Textiles	Garments	12855.34	Large Cap
Raymond Ltd.	Textiles	Clothing	3100.35	Mid Cap
SRF Ltd.	Textiles	Synthetic Fabrics	5000.17	Large Cap
Vardhman Textiles Ltd.	Textiles	Cotton & Blended Yarn	2900.93	Mid Cap
Welspun India Ltd.	Textiles	Synthetic Yarn	3215.64	Mid Cap

MODEL STOCKS PORTFOLIO CONSTRUCTION		Return Expectation	18% CAGR
INVT. AMOUNT (in Rs.)	100000.00	CUSTOMER TYPE	AGGRESSIVE

		MARKET CAP EXPOSURE								
Sector	Companies	Mega Cap	Large Cap	Mid Cap	Small Cap	Micro Cap	Total	CMP (Rs.)	Quantity	Invested Amount (Rs.)
Automobile	Ashok Leyland				4%		4%	23.30	172	4000.00
15%	Bajaj Auto		4%				4%	1800.00	2	4000.00
	Amara Raja			5%			5%	120.00	42	5000.00
	MRF			2%			2%	150.00	13	2000.00
Total		0%	4%	7%	4%	0%	15%			15000.00
Banking	Yes Bank		3%				3%	445.00	7	3000.00
10%	Union Bank			4%			4%	56.00	71	4000.00
	Andhra Bank				3%		3%	100.00	30	3000.00
Total		0%	3%	4%	3%	0%	10%			10000.00
Capital Goods	BHEL		3%				3%	245.00	12	3000.00
10%	Crompton Greaves			4%			4%	124.00	32	4000.00
	Jain Irrigation				3%		3%	234.00	13	3000.00
Total		0%	3%	4%	3%	0%	10%			10000.00
Financial Services	L& T Finance				4%		4%	65.00	62	4000.00
20%	Dewan Housing				4%		4%	345.00	12	4000.00
	India Bulls Fin. Hold			4%			4%	23.00	174	4000.00
	IDFC		4%				4%	145.00	28	4000.00
	Bajaj Finance			4%			4%	124.00	32	4000.00
Total		0%	4%	8%	8%	0%	20%			20000.00

MODEL STOCKS PORTFOLIO CONSTRUCTION	
INVT. AMOUNT (In Rs.)	100000.00

Return Expectation	18% CAGR
CUSTOMER TYPE	AGGRESSIVE

		MARKET CAP EXPOSURE								
Sector	Companies	Mega Cap	Large Cap	Mid Cap	Small Cap	Micro Cap	Total	CMP (Rs.)	Quantity	Invested Amount (Rs.)
FMCG	P & G			4%			4%	345.00	12	4000.00
10%	Dabur India		3%				3%	200.00	15	3000.00
	Colgate Palmolive		3%				3%	1400.00	2	3000.00
Total		0%	6%	4%	0%	0%	10%			10000.00
IT / ITES	NIIT Tech				4%		4%	210.00	19	4000.00
15%	Symphony					5%	5%	143.00	35	5000.00
	Mindtree		3%				3%	670.00	4	3000.00
	Mphasis			3%			3%	455.00	7	3000.00
Total		0%	3%	3%	4%	5%	15%			15000.00
Pharma	Sun Pharma		2%				2%	670.00	3	2000.00
20%	Biocon			5%			5%	345.00	14	5000.00
	Natco Pharma				5%		5%	124.00	40	5000.00
	Sanofi			5%			5%	78.00	64	5000.00
	Kappac Pharma				3%		3%	35.00	86	3000.00
Total		0%	2%	10%	8%	0%	20%			20000.00
GRAND TOTAL		0%	25%	40%	30%	5%	100%			100000.00

AUTOMOBILE	15%
BANKING	10%
CAPITAL GOODS	10%
FINANCIAL SERVICES	20%
FMCG	10%
IT	15%
PHARMA	20%

MEGA CAP	0%
LARGE CAP	25%
MID CAP	40%
SMALL CAP	30%
MICRO CAP	5%

INDICATIVE MARKET CAP EXPOSURE PORTFOLIO DESIGNS

CONSERVATIVE (around 12% compounded portfolio returns)			
Mega & Large Cap	Mid Cap	Small Cap	Micro Cap
80% to 90%	10% to 20%	0%	0%

MODERATELY AGGRESSIVE (around 15% compounded portfolio returns)			
Mega & Large Cap	Mid Cap	Small Cap	Micro Cap
50% to 60%	20% to 30%	10% to 20%	0%

AGGRESSIVE (around 20% compounded portfolio returns)			
Mega & Large Cap	Mid Cap	Small Cap	Micro Cap
30% to 40%	30% to 40%	20% to 25%	10% to 20%

ULTRA AGGRESSIVE (around 25% compounded portfolio returns)			
Mega & Large Cap	Mid Cap	Small Cap	Micro Cap
around 20%	around 30%	around 30%	around 30%
Note: Aggression to the portfolio, as a thumb rule, comes from market cap based exposure to stocks besides choosing some aggressive sectors to achieve aggressive returns. Lower the risk higher would be the exposure to large cap stocks & higher the risk higher would be the exposure to small & micro cap stocks.			

EQUITY MUTUAL FUNDS - SCHEMES & THEMES CLASSIFICATION DATA (as on end Dec 2014)							
				MARKET CAPITALISATION GRID			
Scheme Name	Theme	Launch Date	Since Inception Returns (CAGR)	Mega & Large Cap	Mid Cap	Small & Micro Cap	Debt
AXIS MID CAP FUND	MID CAP ORIENTED	18.02.2011	25.71%	4.00	72.00	24.00	NA
AXIS EQUITY FUND	LARGE CAP ORIENTED	05.01.2010	13.82%	69.00	28.00	3.00	NA
BIRLA SL EQUITY FUND	LARGE & MID CAP ORIENTED	27.08.1998	26.91%	63.00	31.00	6.00	NA
BIRLA SL FRONTLINE EQ. FUND	LARGE CAP ORIENTED	30.08.2002	24.84%	80.00	19.00	1.00	NA
BIRLA SL DIVIDEND YIELD PLUS	MULTICAP (speciality)	26.02.2003	24.99%	50.00	30.00	20.00	NA
BIRLA SL TOP 100 FUND	LARGE & MID CAP ORIENTED	24.10.2005	16.79%	69.00	29.00	2.00	NA
CANARA ROBECO EQ. DIVERSIFIED	LARGE & MID CAP ORIENTED	16.09.2003	21.59%	61.00	32.00	6.00	NA
CANARA ROBECO EMERGING EQ. FUND	MID & SMALL CAP ORIENTED	11.03.2005	18.84%	6.00	53.00	41.00	NA
DSP BR EQUITY FUND	MULTICAP (regular)	29.04.1997	22.14%	48.00	42.00	11.00	NA
DSP BR MICRO CAP	MID, SMALL & MICRO CAP ORIENTED	14.06.2007	18.38%	0.00	30.00	70.00	NA
DSP BR OPPORTUNITIES FUND	MULTICAP (opportunistic)	16.05.2000	19.64%	62.00	25.00	12.00	NA
DSP BR TOP 100 EQ. FUND	LARGE CAP ORIENTED	10.03.2003	26.05%	86.00	13.00	0.00	NA
DSP BR T.I.G.E.R FUND	MULTICAP (Thematic - Infra)	11.06.2004	19.58%	51.00	36.00	13.00	NA
FRANKLIN INDIA BLUECHIP FUND	LARGE CAP ORIENTED	01.12.1993	23.10%	91.00	9.00	0.00	NA
FRANKLIN INDIA PRIMA FUND	MID CAP ORIENTED	01.12.1993	21.58%	22.00	67.00	10.00	NA
FRANKLIN INDIA PRIMA PLUS FUND	LARGE & MID CAP ORIENTED	29.09.1994	20.11%	63.00	32.00	4.00	NA
FRANKLIN INDIA SMALLER COMPANIES	MID & SMALL CAP ORIENTED	13.01.2006	15.20%	14.00	46.00	40.00	NA
FRANKLIN INDIA FLEXICAP FUND	MULTICAP (regular)	02.03.2005	19.61%	70.00	26.00	3.00	NA
FT INDIA BALANCED FUND	EQ. HYBRID / LARGE CAP	10.10.1999	15.23%	DA	DA	DA	27.00
HDFC BALANCED FUND	EQ. HYBRID / LARGE & MID CAP	11.09.2000	17.73%	DA	DA	DA	28.57
HDFC EQUITY FUND	LARGE & MID CAP ORIENTED	01.01.1995	21.12%	72.00	22.00	5.00	NA
HDFC MID-CAP OPP. FUND	MID CAP ORIENTED	25.06.2007	18.18%	19.00	64.00	16.00	NA
HDFC PRUDENCE FUND	EQ. HYBRID / LARGE CAP	01.02.1994	20.50%	38.00	28.00	9.00	25.00
HDFC TOP 200 FUND	LARGE CAP ORIENTED	03.09.1996	22.60%	82.00	16.00	1.00	NA
ICICI PRU FOCUSSED BLUECHIP FUND	LARGE CAP ORIENTED	23.05.2008	17.06%	88.00	12.00	0.00	NA
ICICI PRU BALANCED FUND	EQ. HYBRID / LARGE & MID CAP	03.11.1999	15.48%	49.00	16.00	3.00	32.00
ICICI PRU VALUE DISCOVERY FUND	MID CAP ORIENTED	16.08.2004	25.48%	43.00	43.00	13.00	NA
ICICI PRU DYNAMIC PLAN	MULTICAP (dynamic)	31.10.2002	26.97%	71.00	21.00	6.00	NA
IDFC PREMIER EQUITY FUND	MID & SMALL CAP ORIENTED	15.09.2005	22.67%	24.00	58.00	17.00	NA
IDFC STERLING EQUITY FUND	MID CAP ORIENTED	07.03.2008	20.03%	17.00	65.00	17.00	NA
KOTAK 50 FUND	LARGE CAP ORIENTED	29.12.1998	21.23%	86.00	11.00	1.00	NA

EQUITY MUTUAL FUNDS - SCHEMES & THEMES CLASSIFICATION DATA (as on end Dec 2014)							
				MARKET CAPITALISATION GRID			
Scheme Name	Theme	Launch Date	Since Inception Returns (CAGR)	Mega & Large Cap	Mid Cap	Small & Micro Cap	Debt
KOTAK OPPORTUNITIES FUND	MULTICAP (opportunistic)	09.09.2004	21.92%	70.00	29.00	1.00	NA
KOTAK SELECT FOCUS FUND	LARGE & MID CAP ORIENTED	11.09.2009	15.84%	68.00	28.00	1.00	NA
L&T EQUITY FUND	LARGE CAP ORIENTED	16.05.2005	20.23%	70.00	23.00	6.00	NA
L&T SPECIAL SITUATIONS FUND	MULTICAP (regular)	22.05.2006	15.07%	50.00	42.00	8.00	NA
MIRAE INDIA ASSET OPPR. FUND	LARGE & MID CAP ORIENTED	04.04.2008	18.04%	65.00	25.00	9.00	NA
MIRAE ASSET EMERGING BLUECHIP FUND	MID & SMALL CAP ORIENTED	09.07.2010	25.14%	20.00	57.00	23.00	NA
PRINCIPAL GROWTH FUND	MULTICAP (regular)	25.10.2000	16.88%	60.00	33.00	7.00	NA
PRINCIPAL EMERGING BLUECHIP FUND	MID & SMALL CAP ORIENTED	12.11.2008	35.08%	29.00	58.00	13.00	NA
QUANTUM LONG TERM EQUITY FUND	LARGE & MID CAP ORIENTED	13.03.2006	16.25%	66.00	31.00	3.00	NA
RELIANCE BANKING FUND	SECTOR - BANKING & FIN. SERV.	26.05.2003	27.98%	62.00	36.00	2.00	NA
RELIANCE EQUITY OPP. FUND	MULTICAP (opportunistic)	28.03.2005	22.45%	34.00	58.00	7.00	NA
RELIANCE GROWTH FUND	MULTICAP (regular)	08.10.1995	25.08%	41.00	32.00	26.00	NA
RELIANCE PHARMA FUND (Sector Fund)	MULTI CAP PHARMA / HEALTHCARE	05.06.2004	26.73%	47.00	42.00	10.00	NA
RELIANCE RSF BALANCED FUND	EQ. HYBRID / LARGE CAP	08.06.2005	14.76%	60.00	11.00	4.00	25.00
RELIANCE RSF EQUITY FUND	MULTICAP (regular)	08.06.2005	18.33%	40.00	44.00	15.00	NA
SBI MAGNUM BALANCED FUND	EQ. HYBRID / MULTICAP	31.12.1995	17.40%	34.00	29.00	8.00	29.00
SBI MAGNUM EQUITY FUND	LARGE CAP ORIENTED	01.01.1991	16.07%	85.00	15.00	0.00	NA
SBI MAGNUM GLOBAL FUND	MID & SMALL CAP ORIENTED	30.09.1994	15.66%	7.00	77.00	15.00	NA
SBI MAGNUM MULTIPLIER PLUS	MULTICAP (regular)	01.03.1993	15.01%	57.00	33.00	9.00	NA
SBI EMERGING BUSINESSES FUND	MID & SMALL CAP ORIENTED	11.10.2004	23.65%	8.00	55.00	36.00	NA
SUNDARAM SELECT MID CAP FUND	MID & SMALL CAP ORIENTED	30.07.2002	31.79%	4.00	60.00	25.00	NA
TATA BALANCED FUND	EQ. HYBRID / LARGE CAP ORIENTED	08.10.1995	17.22%	DA	DA	DA	NA
TATA EQUITY OPPORTUNITIES FUND	LARGE & MID CAP ORIENTED	29.03.2003	28.22%	55.00	39.00	5.00	NA
TATA PURE EQUITY FUND	LARGE CAP ORIENTED	07.05.1998	23.64%	84.00	16.00	0.00	NA
UTI EQUITY FUND	LARGE CAP ORIENTED	18.05.1992	12.92%	82.00	14.00	4.00	NA
UTI MASTERSHARE FUND	LARGE CAP ORIENTED	18.10.1986	19.32%	79.00	19.00	2.00	NA
UTI MID CAP FUND	MID & SMALL CAP ORIENTED	07.04.2004	21.51%	16.00	56.00	28.00	NA
UTI OPPORTUNITIES FUND	LARGE CAP (opportunistic)	20.07.2005	17.92%	84.00	15.00	1.00	NA

Note: These are select pure equity and hybrid schemes classified based on its exposure to Mega, Large, Mid, Small & Micro Cap stocks. The schemes has been selected based on the ratings given by www.valueresearchonline.com as on 26th Dec 2014. Most figures are rounded-off. The CAGR returns are compounded annualized since the launch of the respective schemes. Interested investors can identify their respective risk profiles and choose their schemes to invest. Investors can refer the Profiler Chart to understand investment patterns. The ratings for the above are a minimum of 3 stars as seen on www.valueresearchonline.com dated 26.12.2014. Based on this data portfolios in mutual funds can be constructed to meet their investment objectives. Taking of the assistance of a qualified advisor is recommended.

PORTFOLIO CONSTRUCTION IDEAS FOR DIFFERENT INVESTOR RISK PROFILES

Equity Mutual Fund themes including Hybrid themes	Indicative investor suitability (as part of overall portfolio investment portfolio)	Investment Suitability (as part of a portfolio)	Remarks
MONTHLY INCOME PLAN (Debt Hybrid - Debt 75% & Equity 25%)	Conservative	Discretionary	(discretionary)
BALANCED FUNDS (Equity Hybrid - 65% Equity & 35% Debt)	Conservative / Moderately Conservative	Core Portfolio	must have
INDEX FUNDS (exposed to only Sensex / Nifty stocks)	Conservative / Moderately Conservative / Moderately Aggressive	Core Portfolio	must have
LARGE CAP ORIENTED (higher exposure to large cap stocks)	Conservative / Moderately Conservative / Moderately Aggressive / Aggressive	Core Portfolio	must have
MULTI CAP ORIENTED - Regular (exposure to all market caps)	Conservative / Moderately Conservative / Moderately Aggressive / Aggressive	Core Portfolio	must have
MULTI CAP ORIENTED - Opportunistic (exposure to all market caps)	Moderately Aggressive / Aggressive / Ultra Aggressive	Core Portfolio	must have
MID CAP ORIENTED (higher exposure to mid cap stocks)	Moderately Aggressive / Aggressive / Ultra Aggressive	Core Portfolio	must have
SMALL CAP ORIENTED (higher exposure to small cap stocks)	Moderately Aggressive / Aggressive / Ultra Aggressive	Core & Tactical	(discretionary)
MID & SMALL CAP ORIENTED (higher exposure to mid & small cap stocks)	Moderately Aggressive / Aggressive / Ultra Aggressive	Core & Tactical	(discretionary)
SMALL & MID CAP ORIENTED (higher exposure to small & mid cap stocks)	Moderately Aggressive / Aggressive / Ultra Aggressive	Core & Tactical	(discretionary)
MICRO CAP ORIENTED (higher exposure to micro cap stocks)	Aggressive / Ultra Aggressive	Core & Tactical	(discretionary)
THEMATIC SCHEMES (Infra, Services, Power, Consumption etc.)	Aggressive / Ultra Aggressive	Tactial Portfolio	(discretionary)
SECTOR FUNDS (Auto, IT, FMCG, Pharma, Banking etc.)	Aggressive / Ultra Aggressive	Tactial Portfolio	(discretionary)
FUND OF FUNDS (multiple mutual fund schemes)	Conservative / Moderately Conservative / Moderately Aggressive	Tactial Portfolio	(discretionary)
GLOBAL THEMES (exposure to international equity markets)	Moderately Aggressive / Aggressive / Ultra Aggressive	Tactial Portfolio	(discretionary)

Note: Ideally investing in mutual funds should be done as a portfolio. Investors should identify their risk profiles and then choose their suitable themes and start designing their portfolios.

INDICATIVE MUTUAL FUND PORTFOLIOS BASED ON RISK PROFILES

THEMES	PORTFOLIO TYPE	CONSERVATIVE (9% to 12%)	MODERATELY CONS. (12% to 15%)	MODERATELY AGGR. (15% to 18%)	AGGRESSIVE (18% to 25%)	ULTRA AGGR. (25% & ABOVE)
Hybrid Debt (MIP - 75% Equity & 25% Debt)	Core	50%	0%	0%	0%	0%
Balanced Fund	Core	15%	30%	10%	0%	0%
Index Fund	Core	35%	20%	0%	0%	0%
Large Cap oriented	Core	0%	25%	25%	0%	0%
Large & Mid Cap oriented	Core	0%	10%	0%	15%	10%
Multi Cap oriented (regular)	Core	0%	15%	25%	10%	0%
Multi Cap oriented (opportunistic)	Core	0%	0%	15%	20%	20%
Mid Cap oriented	Core	0%	0%	15%	30%	20%
Small Cap oriented	Tactical	0%	0%	0%	0%	0%
Mid & Small Cap oriented	Tactical	0%	0%	10%	25%	25%
Small & Mid Cap oriented	Tactical	0%	0%	0%	0%	15%
Micro Cap oriented	Tactical	0%	0%	0%	0%	0%
Thematic	Tactical	0%	0%	0%	0%	0%
Sector	Tactical	0%	0%	0%	0%	10%
Fund of Funds	Tactical	0%	0%	0%	0%	0%
Global Market Themes	Tactical	0%	0%	0%	0%	0%
		100.00%	100.00%	100.00%	100.00%	100.00%

Note: Core themes are those which can be considered as part of any portfolio. Tactical themes are which are to be included based on the return objective and also risk taking capabilities. Usually tactical themes are suitable for aggressive types of investors. The above themes & percentages are only indicative. Changes can be affected in in consultation with a qualified financial advisor or an investor can do it on his or her own with some basic research work prior to investment.

INDICATIVE MUTUAL FUND PORTFOLIO

Customer Type	Moderately Conservative			
Returns Expected	12% - 15%			
Investment Amount	50000.00			
	Theme Exposure	Scheme Exposure	Theme Value	Scheme Value
BALANCED FUND	30%		15000.00	
ICICI Pru Balanced Fund		15%		7500.00
Reliance RSF Balanced Fund		15%		7500.00
INDEX FUND	30%		15000.00	
HDFC Index Fund - Sensex		15%		7500.00
Franklin India Nifty Plan		15%		7500.00
LARGE CAP	25%		12500.00	
Franklin India Bluechip Fund		10%		5000.00
ICICI Pru Focussed Bluechip Fund		15%		7500.00
MULTICAP	15%		7500.00	
DSP BR Equity Fund		15%		7500.00
TOTAL	**100%**	**100%**	**50000.00**	**50000.00**

INDICATIVE MUTUAL FUND PORTFOLIO				
Customer Type	**Moderately Aggressive**			
Returns Expected	**15% - 18%**			
Investment Amount	**50000.00**			
	Theme Exposure	**Scheme Exposure**	**Theme Value**	**Scheme Value**
BALANCED FUND	10%		5000.00	
HDFC Prudence Fund		10%		5000.00
LARGE CAP	25%		12500.00	
L&T Equity Fund		10%		5000.00
UTI Opportunities Fund		15%		7500.00
MULTICAP (regular)	25%		12500.00	
DSP BR Equity Fund		15%		7500.00
Franklin India Flexi Cap Fund		10%		5000.00
MULTICAP (opportunistic)	15%		7500.00	
Reliance Equity Oppr. Fund		15%		7500.00
MID CAP	15%		7500.00	
ICICI Pru Value Discovery Fund		15%		7500.00
MID & SMALL CAP	10%		5000.00	
SBI Emerging Businesses Fund		10%		5000.00
TOTAL	**100%**	**100%**	**50000.00**	**50000.00**

INDICATIVE MUTUAL FUND PORTFOLIO

Customer Type	**Aggressive**				
Returns Expected	**18% & above**				
Investment Amount	**50000.00**				
	Theme Exposure	**Scheme Exposure**		**Theme Value**	**Scheme Value**
LARGE & MID CAP	15%			7500.00	
Franklin India Prima Plus		15%			7500.00
MULTICAP (regular)	10%			5000.00	
Reliance RSF Equity Fund		10%			5000.00
MULTICAP (opportunistic)	20%			10000.00	
Kotak Opportunities Fund		10%			5000.00
DSP BR Opportunities Fund		10%			5000.00
MID CAP	30%			15000.00	
Sundaram Select Mid Cap Fund		15%			7500.00
HDFC Mid Cap Oppr. Fund		15%			7500.00
MID & SMALL CAP	25%			12500.00	
IDFC Premier Equity Fund		10%			5000.00
Mirae Asset Emerging Bluechip Fund		15%			7500.00
TOTAL	**100%**	**100%**		**50000.00**	**50000.00**

CATEGORY: LARGE CAP ORIENTED						
Date	Franklin India Bluechip Fund (NAV in Rs.)	Amount (Rs.)	Units	Current NAV (Rs.)	Current Value (Rs.)	Profit (Rs.)
7-Dec-93	9.41	1000.00	106.27	340.48	36182.78	35182.78
7-Feb-94	9.93	1000.00	100.70	340.48	34288.02	33288.02
7-Mar-94	13.51	1000.00	74.02	340.48	25202.07	24202.07
7-Apr-94	14.09	1000.00	70.97	340.48	24164.66	23164.66
9-May-94	13.99	1000.00	71.48	340.48	24337.38	23337.38
7-Jun-94	15.15	1000.00	66.01	340.48	22473.93	21473.93
7-Jul-94	16.36	1000.00	61.12	340.48	20811.74	19811.74
8-Aug-94	17.92	1000.00	55.80	340.48	19000.00	18000.00
7-Sep-94	18.76	1000.00	53.30	340.48	18149.25	17149.25
7-Oct-94	18.96	1000.00	52.74	340.48	17957.81	16957.81
7-Nov-94	19.97	1000.00	50.08	340.48	17049.57	16049.57
7-Dec-94	20.46	1000.00	48.88	340.48	16641.25	15641.25
9-Jan-95	19.98	1000.00	50.05	340.48	17041.04	16041.04
7-Feb-95	20.24	1000.00	49.41	340.48	16822.13	15822.13
7-Mar-95	19.96	1000.00	50.10	340.48	17058.12	16058.12
7-Apr-95	20.52	1000.00	48.73	340.48	16592.59	15592.59
8-May-95	18.89	1000.00	52.94	340.48	18024.35	17024.35
7-Jun-95	19.21	1000.00	52.06	340.48	17724.10	16724.10
7-Jul-95	17.58	1000.00	56.88	340.48	19367.46	18367.46
7-Aug-95	18.47	1000.00	54.14	340.48	18434.22	17434.22
7-Sep-95	17.51	1000.00	57.11	340.48	19444.89	18444.89
9-Oct-95	18.05	1000.00	55.40	340.48	18863.16	17863.16
8-Nov-95	16.79	1000.00	59.56	340.48	20278.74	19278.74
7-Dec-95	15.66	1000.00	63.86	340.48	21742.02	20742.02
8-Jan-96	15.30	1000.00	65.36	340.48	22253.59	21253.59
7-Feb-96	14.95	1000.00	66.89	340.48	22774.58	21774.58
7-Mar-96	15.72	1000.00	63.61	340.48	21659.03	20659.03
8-Apr-96	15.30	1000.00	65.36	340.48	22253.59	21253.59
8-May-96	16.33	1000.00	61.24	340.48	20849.97	19849.97
7-Jun-96	15.88	1000.00	62.97	340.48	21440.81	20440.81
8-Jul-96	15.31	1000.00	65.32	340.48	22239.06	21239.06
7-Aug-96	13.72	1000.00	72.89	340.48	24816.33	23816.33
9-Sep-96	13.32	1000.00	75.08	340.48	25561.56	24561.56
7-Oct-96	12.10	1000.00	82.64	340.48	28138.84	27138.84
7-Nov-96	11.95	1000.00	83.68	340.48	28492.05	27492.05
9-Dec-96	11.81	1000.00	84.67	340.48	28829.81	27829.81
31-Jan-97	10.03	1000.00	99.70	340.48	33946.16	32946.16
10-Feb-97	10.03	1000.00	99.70	340.48	33946.16	32946.16
10-Mar-97	10.99	1000.00	90.99	340.48	30980.89	29980.89
7-Apr-97	10.84	1000.00	92.25	340.48	31409.59	30409.59
7-May-97	11.89	1000.00	84.10	340.48	28635.83	27635.83
9-Jun-97	12.42	1000.00	80.52	340.48	27413.85	26413.85
7-Jul-97	13.91	1000.00	71.89	340.48	24477.35	23477.35
7-Aug-97	14.33	1000.00	69.78	340.48	23759.94	22759.94
8-Sep-97	14.39	1000.00	69.49	340.48	23660.88	22660.88

CATEGORY: LARGE CAP ORIENTED						
Date	Franklin India Bluechip Fund (NAV in Rs.)	Amount (Rs.)	Units	Current NAV (Rs.)	Current Value (Rs.)	Profit (Rs.)
7-Oct-97	14.02	1000.00	71.33	340.48	24285.31	23285.31
7-Nov-97	13.61	1000.00	73.48	340.48	25016.90	24016.90
8-Dec-97	13.33	1000.00	75.02	340.48	25542.39	24542.39
7-Jan-98	14.21	1000.00	70.37	340.48	23960.59	22960.59
9-Feb-98	13.84	1000.00	72.25	340.48	24601.16	23601.16
9-Mar-98	15.18	1000.00	65.88	340.48	22429.51	21429.51
7-Apr-98	17.61	1000.00	56.79	340.48	19334.47	18334.47
8-May-98	19.06	1000.00	52.47	340.48	17863.59	16863.59
8-Jun-98	16.61	1000.00	60.20	340.48	20498.49	19498.49
7-Jul-98	16.82	1000.00	59.45	340.48	20242.57	19242.57
7-Aug-98	17.87	1000.00	55.96	340.48	19053.16	18053.16
7-Sep-98	17.76	1000.00	56.31	340.48	19171.17	18171.17
7-Oct-98	18.20	1000.00	54.95	340.48	18707.69	17707.69
9-Nov-98	17.69	1000.00	56.53	340.48	19247.03	18247.03
7-Dec-98	17.76	1000.00	56.31	340.48	19171.17	18171.17
7-Jan-99	19.71	1000.00	50.74	340.48	17274.48	16274.48
8-Feb-99	20.89	1000.00	47.87	340.48	16298.71	15298.71
8-Mar-99	26.07	1000.00	38.36	340.48	13060.22	12060.22
7-Apr-99	26.13	1000.00	38.27	340.48	13030.23	12030.23
7-May-99	25.09	1000.00	39.86	340.48	13570.35	12570.35
7-Jun-99	26.12	1000.00	38.28	340.48	13035.22	12035.22
7-Jul-99	28.24	1000.00	35.41	340.48	12056.66	11056.66
9-Aug-99	31.22	1000.00	32.03	340.48	10905.83	9905.83
7-Sep-99	33.49	1000.00	29.86	340.48	10166.62	9166.62
7-Oct-99	40.36	1000.00	24.78	340.48	8436.08	7436.08
9-Nov-99	38.57	1000.00	25.93	340.48	8827.59	7827.59
7-Dec-99	44.96	1000.00	22.24	340.48	7572.95	6572.95
7-Jan-00	51.35	1000.00	19.47	340.48	6630.57	5630.57
7-Feb-00	56.30	1000.00	17.76	340.48	6047.60	5047.60
7-Mar-00	60.91	1000.00	16.42	340.48	5589.89	4589.89
7-Apr-00	26.29	1000.00	38.04	340.48	12950.93	11950.93
8-May-00	23.77	1000.00	42.07	340.48	14323.94	13323.94
7-Jun-00	24.57	1000.00	40.70	340.48	13857.55	12857.55
7-Jul-00	25.44	1000.00	39.31	340.48	13383.65	12383.65
7-Aug-00	21.56	1000.00	46.38	340.48	15792.21	14792.21
7-Sep-00	24.48	1000.00	40.85	340.48	13908.50	12908.50
9-Oct-00	21.15	1000.00	47.28	340.48	16098.35	15098.35
7-Nov-00	21.85	1000.00	45.77	340.48	15582.61	14582.61
7-Dec-00	23.34	1000.00	42.84	340.48	14587.83	13587.83
8-Jan-01	22.92	1000.00	43.63	340.48	14855.15	13855.15
7-Feb-01	24.25	1000.00	41.24	340.48	14040.41	13040.41
7-Mar-01	22.63	1000.00	44.19	340.48	15045.51	14045.51
9-Apr-01	20.15	1000.00	49.63	340.48	16897.27	15897.27
7-May-01	21.55	1000.00	46.40	340.48	15799.54	14799.54
7-Jun-01	20.81	1000.00	48.05	340.48	16361.36	15361.36

CATEGORY: LARGE CAP ORIENTED						
Date	Franklin India Bluechip Fund (NAV in Rs.)	Amount (Rs.)	Units	Current NAV (Rs.)	Current Value (Rs.)	Profit (Rs.)
9-Jul-01	19.07	1000.00	52.44	340.48	17854.22	16854.22
7-Aug-01	18.97	1000.00	52.71	340.48	17948.34	16948.34
7-Sep-01	18.24	1000.00	54.82	340.48	18666.67	17666.67
8-Oct-01	15.49	1000.00	64.56	340.48	21980.63	20980.63
7-Nov-01	17.73	1000.00	56.40	340.48	19203.61	18203.61
7-Dec-01	19.94	1000.00	50.15	340.48	17075.23	16075.23
7-Jan-02	19.65	1000.00	50.89	340.48	17327.23	16327.23
7-Feb-02	21.59	1000.00	46.32	340.48	15770.26	14770.26
7-Mar-02	24.04	1000.00	41.60	340.48	14163.06	13163.06
8-Apr-02	22.85	1000.00	43.76	340.48	14900.66	13900.66
7-May-02	22.74	1000.00	43.98	340.48	14972.74	13972.74
7-Jun-02	21.64	1000.00	46.21	340.48	15733.83	14733.83
8-Jul-02	23.13	1000.00	43.23	340.48	14720.28	13720.28
7-Aug-02	21.48	1000.00	46.55	340.48	15851.02	14851.02
9-Sep-02	21.08	1000.00	47.44	340.48	16151.80	15151.80
7-Oct-02	20.58	1000.00	48.59	340.48	16544.22	15544.22
7-Nov-02	20.27	1000.00	49.33	340.48	16797.24	15797.24
9-Dec-02	22.35	1000.00	44.74	340.48	15234.00	14234.00
7-Jan-03	23.17	1000.00	43.16	340.48	14694.86	13694.86
7-Feb-03	23.38	1000.00	42.77	340.48	14562.87	13562.87
7-Mar-03	22.52	1000.00	44.40	340.48	15119.01	14119.01
7-Apr-03	23.70	1000.00	42.19	340.48	14366.24	13366.24
7-May-03	23.53	1000.00	42.50	340.48	14470.04	13470.04
9-Jun-03	26.37	1000.00	37.92	340.48	12911.64	11911.64
7-Jul-03	28.65	1000.00	34.90	340.48	11884.12	10884.12
7-Aug-03	31.21	1000.00	32.04	340.48	10909.32	9909.32
8-Sep-03	36.25	1000.00	27.59	340.48	9392.55	8392.55
7-Oct-03	38.19	1000.00	26.18	340.48	8915.42	7915.42
7-Nov-03	42.22	1000.00	23.69	340.48	8064.42	7064.42
8-Dec-03	44.62	1000.00	22.41	340.48	7630.66	6630.66
7-Jan-04	53.65	1000.00	18.64	340.48	6346.32	5346.32
9-Feb-04	53.57	1000.00	18.67	340.48	6355.80	5355.80
8-Mar-04	56.01	1000.00	17.85	340.48	6078.91	5078.91
7-Apr-04	55.48	1000.00	18.02	340.48	6136.99	5136.99
7-May-04	54.00	1000.00	18.52	340.48	6305.19	5305.19
7-Jun-04	47.02	1000.00	21.27	340.48	7241.17	6241.17
7-Jul-04	48.08	1000.00	20.80	340.48	7081.53	6081.53
9-Aug-04	50.48	1000.00	19.81	340.48	6744.85	5744.85
7-Sep-04	51.42	1000.00	19.45	340.48	6621.55	5621.55
7-Oct-04	54.81	1000.00	18.24	340.48	6212.01	5212.01
8-Nov-04	55.67	1000.00	17.96	340.48	6116.04	5116.04
7-Dec-04	60.15	1000.00	16.63	340.48	5660.52	4660.52
7-Jan-05	62.19	1000.00	16.08	340.48	5474.84	4474.84
7-Feb-05	63.58	1000.00	15.73	340.48	5355.14	4355.14
7-Mar-05	66.58	1000.00	15.02	340.48	5113.85	4113.85

CATEGORY: LARGE CAP ORIENTED						
Date	Franklin India Bluechip Fund (NAV in Rs.)	Amount (Rs.)	Units	Current NAV (Rs.)	Current Value (Rs.)	Profit (Rs.)
1-Apr-05	64.06	1000.00	15.61	340.48	5315.02	4315.02
9-May-05	62.51	1000.00	16.00	340.48	5446.81	4446.81
7-Jun-05	64.55	1000.00	15.49	340.48	5274.67	4274.67
7-Jul-05	67.51	1000.00	14.81	340.48	5043.40	4043.40
8-Aug-05	73.87	1000.00	13.54	340.48	4609.18	3609.18
8-Sep-05	79.38	1000.00	12.60	340.48	4289.24	3289.24
7-Oct-05	82.45	1000.00	12.13	340.48	4129.53	3129.53
7-Nov-05	79.00	1000.00	12.66	340.48	4309.87	3309.87
7-Dec-05	86.89	1000.00	11.51	340.48	3918.52	2918.52
9-Jan-06	93.35	1000.00	10.71	340.48	3647.35	2647.35
7-Feb-06	99.34	1000.00	10.07	340.48	3427.42	2427.42
7-Mar-06	106.99	1000.00	9.35	340.48	3182.35	2182.35
7-Apr-06	115.92	1000.00	8.63	340.48	2937.20	1937.20
8-May-06	122.44	1000.00	8.17	340.48	2780.79	1780.79
7-Jun-06	94.27	1000.00	10.61	340.48	3611.75	2611.75
7-Jul-06	99.20	1000.00	10.08	340.48	3432.26	2432.26
7-Aug-06	102.06	1000.00	9.80	340.48	3336.08	2336.08
7-Sep-06	113.89	1000.00	8.78	340.48	2989.55	1989.55
9-Oct-06	118.45	1000.00	8.44	340.48	2874.46	1874.46
7-Nov-06	125.82	1000.00	7.95	340.48	2706.09	1706.09
7-Dec-06	132.23	1000.00	7.56	340.48	2574.91	1574.91
8-Jan-07	129.22	1000.00	7.74	340.48	2634.89	1634.89
7-Feb-07	139.63	1000.00	7.16	340.48	2438.44	1438.44
7-Mar-07	117.72	1000.00	8.49	340.48	2892.29	1892.29
9-Apr-07	123.98	1000.00	8.07	340.48	2746.17	1746.17
7-May-07	131.85	1000.00	7.58	340.48	2582.28	1582.28
7-Jun-07	135.90	1000.00	7.36	340.48	2505.43	1505.43
9-Jul-07	145.74	1000.00	6.86	340.48	2336.19	1336.19
7-Aug-07	146.98	1000.00	6.80	340.48	2316.55	1316.55
7-Sep-07	150.48	1000.00	6.65	340.48	2262.66	1262.66
8-Oct-07	166.94	1000.00	5.99	340.48	2039.52	1039.52
7-Nov-07	177.95	1000.00	5.62	340.48	1913.34	913.34
7-Dec-07	190.08	1000.00	5.26	340.48	1791.29	791.29
7-Jan-08	195.58	1000.00	5.11	340.48	1740.87	740.87
7-Feb-08	163.60	1000.00	6.11	340.48	2081.15	1081.15
7-Mar-08	150.13	1000.00	6.66	340.48	2267.87	1267.87
7-Apr-08	145.50	1000.00	6.87	340.48	2339.99	1339.99
7-May-08	158.44	1000.00	6.31	340.48	2148.96	1148.96
9-Jun-08	141.04	1000.00	7.09	340.48	2413.98	1413.98
7-Jul-08	126.70	1000.00	7.89	340.48	2687.24	1687.24
7-Aug-08	141.64	1000.00	7.06	340.48	2403.85	1403.85
8-Sep-08	140.89	1000.00	7.10	340.48	2416.72	1416.72
7-Oct-08	118.28	1000.00	8.45	340.48	2878.65	1878.65
7-Nov-08	102.58	1000.00	9.75	340.48	3319.24	2319.24
8-Dec-08	95.65	1000.00	10.46	340.48	3559.82	2559.82

CATEGORY: LARGE CAP ORIENTED						
Date	Franklin India Bluechip Fund (NAV in Rs.)	Amount (Rs.)	Units	Current NAV (Rs.)	Current Value (Rs.)	Profit (Rs.)
7-Jan-09	100.76	1000.00	9.92	340.48	3379.17	2379.17
9-Feb-09	99.06	1000.00	10.09	340.48	3437.13	2437.13
9-Mar-09	87.67	1000.00	11.41	340.48	3883.70	2883.70
8-Apr-09	109.84	1000.00	9.10	340.48	3099.76	2099.76
7-May-09	123.92	1000.00	8.07	340.48	2747.52	1747.52
8-Jun-09	148.41	1000.00	6.74	340.48	2294.11	1294.11
7-Jul-09	149.04	1000.00	6.71	340.48	2284.56	1284.56
7-Aug-09	156.98	1000.00	6.37	340.48	2168.94	1168.94
7-Sep-09	165.66	1000.00	6.04	340.48	2055.29	1055.29
7-Oct-09	172.69	1000.00	5.79	340.48	1971.63	971.63
9-Nov-09	174.34	1000.00	5.74	340.48	1952.97	952.97
7-Dec-09	180.66	1000.00	5.54	340.48	1884.65	884.65
7-Jan-10	187.87	1000.00	5.32	340.48	1812.32	812.32
8-Feb-10	187.87	1000.00	5.32	340.48	1812.32	812.32
8-Mar-10	189.31	1000.00	5.28	340.48	1798.53	798.53
7-Apr-10	196.13	1000.00	5.10	340.48	1735.99	735.99
7-May-10	186.16	1000.00	5.37	340.48	1828.96	828.96
7-Jun-10	187.95	1000.00	5.32	340.48	1811.55	811.55
7-Jul-10	195.29	1000.00	5.12	340.48	1743.46	743.46
9-Aug-10	205.77	1000.00	4.86	340.48	1654.66	654.66
7-Sep-10	211.16	1000.00	4.74	340.48	1612.43	612.43
7-Oct-10	226.81	1000.00	4.41	340.48	1501.17	501.17
7-Nov-10	228.72	1000.00	4.37	340.48	1488.63	488.63
7-Dec-10	224.24	1000.00	4.46	340.48	1518.37	518.37
7-Jan-11	221.97	1000.00	4.51	340.48	1533.90	533.90
7-Feb-11	205.66	1000.00	4.86	340.48	1655.55	655.55
7-Mar-11	206.88	1000.00	4.83	340.48	1645.78	645.78
7-Apr-11	221.54	1000.00	4.51	340.48	1536.88	536.88
9-May-11	213.25	1000.00	4.69	340.48	1596.62	596.62
7-Jun-11	214.46	1000.00	4.66	340.48	1587.62	587.62
7-Jul-11	219.86	1000.00	4.55	340.48	1548.62	548.62
8-Aug-11	202.46	1000.00	4.94	340.48	1681.71	681.71
8-Sep-11	203.70	1000.00	4.91	340.48	1671.48	671.48
7-Oct-11	194.92	1000.00	5.13	340.48	1746.77	746.77
8-Nov-11	209.03	1000.00	4.78	340.48	1628.86	628.86
7-Dec-11	200.80	1000.00	4.98	340.48	1695.62	695.62
7-Jan-12	189.55	1000.00	5.28	340.48	1796.25	796.25
7-Feb-12	212.52	1000.00	4.71	340.48	1602.11	602.11
7-Mar-12	209.87	1000.00	4.76	340.48	1622.34	622.34
9-Apr-12	211.49	1000.00	4.73	340.48	1609.91	609.91
7-May-12	203.95	1000.00	4.90	340.48	1669.43	669.43
7-Jun-12	201.65	1000.00	4.96	340.48	1688.47	688.47
9-Jul-12	211.36	1000.00	4.73	340.48	1610.90	610.90
7-Aug-12	213.16	1000.00	4.69	340.48	1597.30	597.30
7-Sep-12	212.13	1000.00	4.71	340.48	1605.05	605.05

CATEGORY: LARGE CAP ORIENTED						
Date	Franklin India Bluechip Fund (NAV in Rs.)	Amount (Rs.)	Units	Current NAV (Rs.)	Current Value (Rs.)	Profit (Rs.)
8-Oct-12	223.24	1000.00	4.48	340.48	1525.17	525.17
7-Nov-12	225.50	1000.00	4.43	340.48	1509.89	509.89
7-Dec-12	233.63	1000.00	4.28	340.48	1457.35	457.35
7-Jan-13	240.71	1000.00	4.15	340.48	1414.48	414.48
7-Feb-13	237.78	1000.00	4.21	340.48	1431.91	431.91
7-Mar-13	234.91	1000.00	4.26	340.48	1449.41	449.41
8-Apr-13	223.10	1000.00	4.48	340.48	1526.13	526.13
7-May-13	237.35	1000.00	4.21	340.48	1434.51	434.51
7-Jun-13	231.47	1000.00	4.32	340.48	1470.95	470.95
8-Jul-13	225.59	1000.00	4.43	340.48	1509.29	509.29
8-Aug-13	213.37	1000.00	4.69	340.48	1595.73	595.73
10-Sep-13	225.82	1000.00	4.43	340.48	1507.75	507.75
8-Oct-13	228.15	1000.00	4.38	340.48	1492.35	492.35
7-Nov-13	241.39	1000.00	4.14	340.48	1410.50	410.50
7-Dec-13	245.07	1000.00	4.08	340.48	1389.32	389.32
7-Jan-14	241.25	1000.00	4.15	340.48	1411.32	411.32
7-Feb-14	237.43	1000.00	4.21	340.48	1434.02	434.02
7-Mar-14	252.98	1000.00	3.95	340.48	1345.88	345.88
7-Apr-14	260.13	1000.00	3.84	340.48	1308.88	308.88
7-May-14	257.35	1000.00	3.89	340.48	1323.02	323.02
6-Jun-14	295.29	1000.00	3.39	340.48	1153.04	153.04
7-Jul-14	303.36	1000.00	3.30	340.48	1122.36	122.36
7-Aug-14	299.05	1000.00	3.34	340.48	1138.54	138.54
8-Sep-14	323.64	1000.00	3.09	340.48	1052.03	52.03
7-Oct-14	311.40	1000.00	3.21	340.48	1093.38	93.38
7-Nov-14	336.04	1000.00	2.98	340.48	1013.21	13.21
8-Dec-14	340.48	1000.00	2.94	340.48	1000.00	0.00
	TOTAL	252000.00	7483.11		2547848.29	2295848.29

CATEGORY: MID CAP ORIENTED						
Date	Franklin India Prima Fund (NAV in Rs.)	Amount (Rs.)	Units	Current NAV (Rs.)	Current Value (Rs.)	Profit (Rs.)
23-Dec-93	10.41	1000	96.06	611.63	58754.08	57754.08
20-Jan-94	11.43	1000	87.49	611.63	53510.94	52510.94
21-Feb-94	12.32	1000	81.17	611.63	49645.29	48645.29
21-Mar-94	15.07	1000	66.36	611.63	40585.93	39585.93
20-Apr-94	14.65	1000	68.26	611.63	41749.49	40749.49
20-May-94	14.93	1000	66.98	611.63	40966.51	39966.51
20-Jun-94	16.15	1000	61.92	611.63	37871.83	36871.83
20-Jul-94	16.60	1000	60.24	611.63	36845.18	35845.18
22-Aug-94	18.72	1000	53.42	611.63	32672.54	31672.54
20-Sep-94	20.11	1000	49.73	611.63	30414.22	29414.22
20-Oct-94	20.19	1000	49.53	611.63	30293.71	29293.71
22-Nov-94	20.46	1000	48.88	611.63	29893.94	28893.94
20-Dec-94	20.27	1000	49.33	611.63	30174.15	29174.15
20-Jan-95	18.88	1000	52.97	611.63	32395.66	31395.66
20-Feb-95	17.69	1000	56.53	611.63	34574.90	33574.90
20-Mar-95	17.97	1000	55.65	611.63	34036.17	33036.17
20-Apr-95	17.86	1000	55.99	611.63	34245.80	33245.80
22-May-95	17.07	1000	58.58	611.63	35830.70	34830.70
20-Jun-95	17.38	1000	57.54	611.63	35191.60	34191.60
20-Jul-95	17.15	1000	58.31	611.63	35663.56	34663.56
21-Aug-95	16.72	1000	59.81	611.63	36580.74	35580.74
20-Sep-95	15.61	1000	64.06	611.63	39181.93	38181.93
20-Oct-95	15.61	1000	64.06	611.63	39181.93	38181.93
20-Nov-95	13.97	1000	71.58	611.63	43781.68	42781.68
20-Dec-95	13.43	1000	74.46	611.63	45542.07	44542.07
22-Jan-96	12.30	1000	81.30	611.63	49726.02	48726.02
20-Feb-96	14.85	1000	67.34	611.63	41187.21	40187.21
21-Mar-96	14.02	1000	71.33	611.63	43625.53	42625.53
22-Apr-96	14.32	1000	69.83	611.63	42711.59	41711.59
20-May-96	13.76	1000	72.67	611.63	44449.85	43449.85
20-Jun-96	13.33	1000	75.02	611.63	45883.72	44883.72
22-Jul-96	12.82	1000	78.00	611.63	47709.05	46709.05
20-Aug-96	10.87	1000	92.00	611.63	56267.71	55267.71
20-Sep-96	10.95	1000	91.32	611.63	55856.62	54856.62
22-Oct-96	10.25	1000	97.56	611.63	59671.22	58671.22
20-Nov-96	9.73	1000	102.77	611.63	62860.23	61860.23
20-Dec-96	9.71	1000	102.99	611.63	62989.70	61989.70
20-Jan-97	11.73	1000	85.25	611.63	52142.37	51142.37
20-Feb-97	10.73	1000	93.20	611.63	57001.86	56001.86
20-Mar-97	10.49	1000	95.33	611.63	58306.01	57306.01
21-Apr-97	10.61	1000	94.25	611.63	57646.56	56646.56
20-May-97	9.65	1000	103.63	611.63	63381.35	62381.35
20-Jun-97	10.41	1000	96.06	611.63	58754.08	57754.08
21-Jul-97	10.42	1000	95.97	611.63	58697.70	57697.70
20-Aug-97	10.33	1000	96.81	611.63	59209.10	58209.10

CATEGORY: MID CAP ORIENTED						
Date	Franklin India Prima Fund (NAV in Rs.)	Amount (Rs.)	Units	Current NAV (Rs.)	Current Value (Rs.)	Profit (Rs.)
22-Sep-97	9.57	1000	104.49	611.63	63911.18	62911.18
20-Oct-97	9.51	1000	105.15	611.63	64314.41	63314.41
20-Nov-97	8.73	1000	114.55	611.63	70060.71	69060.71
22-Dec-97	8.90	1000	112.36	611.63	68722.47	67722.47
20-Jan-98	9.06	1000	110.38	611.63	67508.83	66508.83
20-Feb-98	9.07	1000	110.25	611.63	67434.40	66434.40
20-Mar-98	9.74	1000	102.67	611.63	62795.69	61795.69
20-Apr-98	12.18	1000	82.10	611.63	50215.93	49215.93
20-May-98	12.19	1000	82.03	611.63	50174.73	49174.73
22-Jun-98	9.06	1000	110.38	611.63	67508.83	66508.83
20-Jul-98	10.53	1000	94.97	611.63	58084.52	57084.52
20-Aug-98	10.30	1000	97.09	611.63	59381.55	58381.55
21-Sep-98	10.52	1000	95.06	611.63	58139.73	57139.73
20-Oct-98	10.65	1000	93.90	611.63	57430.05	56430.05
20-Nov-98	11.10	1000	90.09	611.63	55101.80	54101.80
21-Dec-98	11.48	1000	87.11	611.63	53277.87	52277.87
21-Jan-99	13.41	1000	74.57	611.63	45609.99	44609.99
22-Feb-99	13.95	1000	71.68	611.63	43844.44	42844.44
22-Mar-99	17.20	1000	58.14	611.63	35559.88	34559.88
20-Apr-99	14.56	1000	68.68	611.63	42007.55	41007.55
20-May-99	14.92	1000	67.02	611.63	40993.97	39993.97
21-Jun-99	14.88	1000	67.20	611.63	41104.17	40104.17
20-Jul-99	17.59	1000	56.85	611.63	34771.46	33771.46
20-Aug-99	20.62	1000	48.50	611.63	29661.98	28661.98
20-Sep-99	22.58	1000	44.29	611.63	27087.25	26087.25
20-Oct-99	28.54	1000	35.04	611.63	21430.62	20430.62
22-Nov-99	28.04	1000	35.66	611.63	21812.77	20812.77
20-Dec-99	32.90	1000	30.40	611.63	18590.58	17590.58
20-Jan-00	36.20	1000	27.62	611.63	16895.86	15895.86
21-Feb-00	40.82	1000	24.50	611.63	14983.59	13983.59
21-Mar-00	29.75	1000	33.61	611.63	20558.99	19558.99
20-Apr-00	25.47	1000	39.26	611.63	24013.74	23013.74
22-May-00	21.38	1000	46.77	611.63	28607.58	27607.58
20-Jun-00	24.30	1000	41.15	611.63	25169.96	24169.96
20-Jul-00	22.65	1000	44.15	611.63	27003.53	26003.53
21-Aug-00	21.83	1000	45.81	611.63	28017.87	27017.87
20-Sep-00	22.00	1000	45.45	611.63	27801.36	26801.36
20-Oct-00	19.24	1000	51.98	611.63	31789.50	30789.50
20-Nov-00	19.24	1000	51.98	611.63	31789.50	30789.50
20-Dec-00	20.60	1000	48.54	611.63	29690.78	28690.78
22-Jan-01	20.92	1000	47.80	611.63	29236.62	28236.62
20-Feb-01	24.71	1000	40.47	611.63	24752.33	23752.33
20-Mar-01	19.02	1000	52.58	611.63	32157.20	31157.20
20-Apr-01	18.31	1000	54.61	611.63	33404.15	32404.15
21-May-01	19.27	1000	51.89	611.63	31740.01	30740.01

CATEGORY: MID CAP ORIENTED						
Date	Franklin India Prima Fund (NAV in Rs.)	Amount (Rs.)	Units	Current NAV (Rs.)	Current Value (Rs.)	Profit (Rs.)
20-Jun-01	18.32	1000	54.59	611.63	33385.92	32385.92
20-Jul-01	16.98	1000	58.89	611.63	36020.61	35020.61
20-Aug-01	16.44	1000	60.83	611.63	37203.77	36203.77
20-Sep-01	14.35	1000	69.69	611.63	42622.30	41622.30
22-Oct-01	16.15	1000	61.92	611.63	37871.83	36871.83
20-Nov-01	19.26	1000	51.92	611.63	31756.49	30756.49
20-Dec-01	19.80	1000	50.51	611.63	30890.40	29890.40
21-Jan-02	21.49	1000	46.53	611.63	28461.14	27461.14
20-Feb-02	25.15	1000	39.76	611.63	24319.28	23319.28
20-Mar-02	26.24	1000	38.11	611.63	23309.07	22309.07
22-Apr-02	26.94	1000	37.12	611.63	22703.41	21703.41
20-May-02	26.53	1000	37.69	611.63	23054.28	22054.28
20-Jun-02	29.21	1000	34.23	611.63	20939.06	19939.06
22-Jul-02	28.50	1000	35.09	611.63	21460.70	20460.70
20-Aug-02	27.34	1000	36.58	611.63	22371.25	21371.25
20-Sep-02	26.97	1000	37.08	611.63	22678.16	21678.16
21-Oct-02	27.07	1000	36.94	611.63	22594.38	21594.38
20-Nov-02	26.90	1000	37.17	611.63	22737.17	21737.17
20-Dec-02	28.22	1000	35.44	611.63	21673.64	20673.64
20-Jan-03	29.91	1000	33.43	611.63	20449.01	19449.01
20-Feb-03	29.60	1000	33.78	611.63	20663.18	19663.18
20-Mar-03	28.55	1000	35.03	611.63	21423.12	20423.12
21-Apr-03	30.01	1000	33.32	611.63	20380.87	19380.87
20-May-03	34.95	1000	28.61	611.63	17500.14	16500.14
20-Jun-03	39.63	1000	25.23	611.63	15433.51	14433.51
21-Jul-03	43.23	1000	23.13	611.63	14148.28	13148.28
20-Aug-03	48.41	1000	20.66	611.63	12634.37	11634.37
22-Sep-03	48.71	1000	20.53	611.63	12556.56	11556.56
20-Oct-03	56.24	1000	17.78	611.63	10875.36	9875.36
20-Nov-03	60.15	1000	16.63	611.63	10168.41	9168.41
22-Dec-03	78.36	1000	12.76	611.63	7805.39	6805.39
20-Jan-04	78.89	1000	12.68	611.63	7752.95	6752.95
20-Feb-04	74.95	1000	13.34	611.63	8160.51	7160.51
22-Mar-04	67.01	1000	14.92	611.63	9127.44	8127.44
20-Apr-04	78.52	1000	12.74	611.63	7789.48	6789.48
20-May-04	71.35	1000	14.02	611.63	8572.25	7572.25
21-Jun-04	67.59	1000	14.80	611.63	9049.12	8049.12
20-Jul-04	75.11	1000	13.31	611.63	8143.12	7143.12
20-Aug-04	76.77	1000	13.03	611.63	7967.04	6967.04
20-Sep-04	83.80	1000	11.93	611.63	7298.69	6298.69
20-Oct-04	87.07	1000	11.49	611.63	7024.58	6024.58
22-Nov-04	95.79	1000	10.44	611.63	6385.11	5385.11
20-Dec-04	104.25	1000	9.59	611.63	5866.95	4866.95
20-Jan-05	104.34	1000	9.58	611.63	5861.89	4861.89
21-Feb-05	115.25	1000	8.68	611.63	5306.98	4306.98

CATEGORY: MID CAP ORIENTED						
Date	Franklin India Prima Fund (NAV in Rs.)	Amount (Rs.)	Units	Current NAV (Rs.)	Current Value (Rs.)	Profit (Rs.)
21-Mar-05	116.36	1000	8.59	611.63	5256.36	4256.36
20-Apr-05	114.63	1000	8.72	611.63	5335.69	4335.69
20-May-05	124.51	1000	8.03	611.63	4912.30	3912.30
20-Jun-05	122.92	1000	8.14	611.63	4975.84	3975.84
20-Jul-05	136.22	1000	7.34	611.63	4490.02	3490.02
22-Aug-05	149.55	1000	6.69	611.63	4089.80	3089.80
20-Sep-05	160.08	1000	6.25	611.63	3820.78	2820.78
20-Oct-05	148.43	1000	6.74	611.63	4120.66	3120.66
21-Nov-05	160.03	1000	6.25	611.63	3821.97	2821.97
20-Dec-05	171.16	1000	5.84	611.63	3573.44	2573.44
20-Jan-06	180.94	1000	5.53	611.63	3380.29	2380.29
20-Feb-06	180.59	1000	5.54	611.63	3386.84	2386.84
20-Mar-06	190.91	1000	5.24	611.63	3203.76	2203.76
20-Apr-06	202.05	1000	4.95	611.63	3027.12	2027.12
22-May-06	179.14	1000	5.58	611.63	3414.26	2414.26
20-Jun-06	153.11	1000	6.53	611.63	3994.71	2994.71
21-Jul-06	150.05	1000	6.66	611.63	4076.17	3076.17
21-Aug-06	175.39	1000	5.70	611.63	3487.26	2487.26
20-Sep-06	181.44	1000	5.51	611.63	3370.98	2370.98
20-Oct-06	189.64	1000	5.27	611.63	3225.22	2225.22
20-Nov-06	197.23	1000	5.07	611.63	3101.10	2101.10
20-Dec-06	204.34	1000	4.89	611.63	2993.20	1993.20
22-Jan-07	220.24	1000	4.54	611.63	2777.11	1777.11
20-Feb-07	208.78	1000	4.79	611.63	2929.54	1929.54
20-Mar-07	185.55	1000	5.39	611.63	3296.31	2296.31
20-Apr-07	195.59	1000	5.11	611.63	3127.05	2127.05
21-May-07	205.91	1000	4.86	611.63	2970.41	1970.41
20-Jun-07	219.15	1000	4.56	611.63	2790.94	1790.94
20-Jul-07	234.47	1000	4.26	611.63	2608.55	1608.55
20-Aug-07	220.23	1000	4.54	611.63	2777.25	1777.25
20-Sep-07	242.58	1000	4.12	611.63	2521.37	1521.37
22-Oct-07	241.07	1000	4.15	611.63	2537.19	1537.19
20-Nov-07	277.88	1000	3.60	611.63	2201.09	1201.09
20-Dec-07	291.65	1000	3.43	611.63	2097.17	1097.17
21-Jan-08	257.66	1000	3.88	611.63	2373.78	1373.78
20-Feb-08	241.19	1000	4.15	611.63	2535.91	1535.91
24-Mar-08	185.11	1000	5.40	611.63	3304.20	2304.20
21-Apr-08	216.69	1000	4.61	611.63	2822.65	1822.65
20-May-08	217.18	1000	4.60	611.63	2816.20	1816.20
20-Jun-08	184.29	1000	5.43	611.63	3318.76	2318.76
21-Jul-08	168.00	1000	5.95	611.63	3640.62	2640.62
20-Aug-08	183.39	1000	5.45	611.63	3335.12	2335.12
22-Sep-08	173.32	1000	5.77	611.63	3528.87	2528.87
20-Oct-08	128.97	1000	7.75	611.63	4742.24	3742.24
20-Nov-08	106.49	1000	9.39	611.63	5743.81	4743.81

CATEGORY: MID CAP ORIENTED						
Date	Franklin India Prima Fund (NAV in Rs.)	Amount (Rs.)	Units	Current NAV (Rs.)	Current Value (Rs.)	Profit (Rs.)
22-Dec-08	119.33	1000	8.38	611.63	5125.49	4125.49
20-Jan-09	112.36	1000	8.90	611.63	5443.57	4443.57
20-Feb-09	104.79	1000	9.54	611.63	5836.62	4836.62
20-Mar-09	102.28	1000	9.78	611.63	5980.21	4980.21
20-Apr-09	126.82	1000	7.89	611.63	4822.86	3822.86
20-May-09	165.40	1000	6.05	611.63	3697.85	2697.85
22-Jun-09	171.37	1000	5.84	611.63	3569.16	2569.16
20-Jul-09	184.87	1000	5.41	611.63	3308.43	2308.43
20-Aug-09	192.55	1000	5.19	611.63	3176.47	2176.47
20-Sep-09	206.64	1000	4.84	611.63	2959.88	1959.88
20-Oct-09	231.40	1000	4.32	611.63	2643.17	1643.17
20-Nov-09	232.58	1000	4.30	611.63	2629.76	1629.76
21-Dec-09	236.37	1000	4.23	611.63	2587.60	1587.60
20-Jan-10	257.98	1000	3.88	611.63	2370.84	1370.84
22-Feb-10	234.50	1000	4.26	611.63	2608.23	1608.23
22-Mar-10	252.65	1000	3.96	611.63	2420.86	1420.86
20-Apr-10	259.31	1000	3.86	611.63	2358.68	1358.68
20-May-10	247.12	1000	4.05	611.63	2475.03	1475.03
20-Jun-10	261.59	1000	3.82	611.63	2338.12	1338.12
20-Jul-10	272.72	1000	3.67	611.63	2242.70	1242.70
20-Aug-10	286.77	1000	3.49	611.63	2132.86	1132.86
20-Sep-10	296.74	1000	3.37	611.63	2061.16	1061.16
20-Nov-10	301.23	1000	3.32	611.63	2030.44	1030.44
20-Dec-10	286.23	1000	3.49	611.63	2136.85	1136.85
20-Jan-11	271.04	1000	3.69	611.63	2256.60	1256.60
21-Feb-11	255.91	1000	3.91	611.63	2390.02	1390.02
21-Mar-11	251.50	1000	3.98	611.63	2431.93	1431.93
20-Apr-11	275.77	1000	3.63	611.63	2217.90	1217.90
20-May-11	267.64	1000	3.74	611.63	2285.27	1285.27
20-Jun-11	267.21	1000	3.74	611.63	2288.95	1288.95
20-Jul-11	274.91	1000	3.64	611.63	2224.84	1224.84
19-Aug-11	249.54	1000	4.01	611.63	2451.03	1451.03
20-Sep-11	257.74	1000	3.88	611.63	2373.05	1373.05
20-Oct-11	253.51	1000	3.94	611.63	2412.65	1412.65
21-Nov-11	241.32	1000	4.14	611.63	2534.52	1534.52
20-Dec-11	224.70	1000	4.45	611.63	2721.98	1721.98
20-Jan-12	242.99	1000	4.12	611.63	2517.10	1517.10
21-Feb-12	269.02	1000	3.72	611.63	2273.55	1273.55
20-Mar-12	264.82	1000	3.78	611.63	2309.61	1309.61
20-Apr-12	270.82	1000	3.69	611.63	2258.44	1258.44
21-May-12	254.40	1000	3.93	611.63	2404.21	1404.21
20-Jun-12	256.70	1000	3.90	611.63	2382.66	1382.66
20-Jul-12	268.58	1000	3.72	611.63	2277.27	1277.27
21-Aug-12	274.59	1000	3.64	611.63	2227.43	1227.43
20-Sep-12	280.85	1000	3.56	611.63	2177.78	1177.78

CATEGORY: MID CAP ORIENTED						
Date	Franklin India Prima Fund (NAV in Rs.)	Amount (Rs.)	Units	Current NAV (Rs.)	Current Value (Rs.)	Profit (Rs.)
22-Oct-12	301.07	1000	3.32	611.63	2031.52	1031.52
20-Nov-12	300.00	1000	3.33	611.63	2038.77	1038.77
20-Dec-12	325.40	1000	3.07	611.63	1879.63	879.63
21-Jan-13	330.59	1000	3.02	611.63	1850.12	850.12
20-Feb-13	321.27	1000	3.11	611.63	1903.79	903.79
20-Mar-13	303.65	1000	3.29	611.63	2014.26	1014.26
22-Apr-13	307.90	1000	3.25	611.63	1986.46	986.46
20-May-13	324.17	1000	3.08	611.63	1886.76	886.76
20-Jun-13	315.03	1000	3.17	611.63	1941.50	941.50
19-Jul-13	320.58	1000	3.12	611.63	1907.89	907.89
20-Aug-13	285.01	1000	3.51	611.63	2145.99	1145.99
20-Sep-13	308.17	1000	3.24	611.63	1984.72	984.72
21-Oct-13	321.15	1000	3.11	611.63	1904.50	904.50
21-Nov-13	329.72	1000	3.03	611.63	1855.00	855.00
21-Dec-13	348.70	1000	2.87	611.63	1754.03	754.03
21-Jan-14	348.14	1000	2.87	611.63	1756.85	756.85
20-Feb-14	347.54	1000	2.88	611.63	1759.88	759.88
20-Mar-14	346.10	1000	2.89	611.63	1767.21	767.21
21-Apr-14	405.19	1000	2.47	611.63	1509.49	509.49
20-May-14	448.44	1000	2.23	611.63	1363.91	363.91
20-Jun-14	481.06	1000	2.08	611.63	1271.42	271.42
21-Jul-14	503.67	1000	1.99	611.63	1214.35	214.35
21-Aug-14	522.37	1000	1.91	611.63	1170.88	170.88
20-Sep-14	561.34	1000	1.78	611.63	1089.59	89.59
20-Oct-14	543.20	1000	1.84	611.63	1125.98	125.98
20-Nov-14	599.34	1000	1.67	611.63	1020.51	20.51
19-Dec-14	611.63	1000	1.63	611.63	1000.00	0.00
	TOTAL	252000	8197.07		5013571.67	4761571.67

CATEGORY: LARGE & MID-CAP ORIENTED						
Date	HDFC Equity Fund (NAV in Rs.)	Amount (Rs.)	Units	Current NAV (Rs.)	Current Value (Rs.)	Profit (Rs.)
10-Jan-95	9.29	1000.00	107.64	471.27	50728.74	49728.74
10-Feb-95	9.24	1000.00	108.23	471.27	51003.25	50003.25
10-Mar-95	9.23	1000.00	108.34	471.27	51058.50	50058.50
19-Apr-95	9.24	1000.00	108.23	471.27	51003.25	50003.25
10-May-95	8.91	1000.00	112.23	471.27	52892.26	51892.26
12-Jun-95	9.02	1000.00	110.86	471.27	52247.23	51247.23
10-Jul-95	8.49	1000.00	117.79	471.27	55508.83	54508.83
10-Aug-95	8.33	1000.00	120.05	471.27	56575.03	55575.03
11-Sep-95	8.06	1000.00	124.07	471.27	58470.22	57470.22
10-Oct-95	8.46	1000.00	118.20	471.27	55705.67	54705.67
10-Nov-95	7.56	1000.00	132.28	471.27	62337.30	61337.30
11-Dec-95	7.19	1000.00	139.08	471.27	65545.20	64545.20
10-Jan-96	6.84	1000.00	146.20	471.27	68899.12	67899.12
12-Feb-96	7.10	1000.00	140.85	471.27	66376.06	65376.06
11-Mar-96	7.11	1000.00	140.65	471.27	66282.70	65282.70
10-Apr-96	7.22	1000.00	138.50	471.27	65272.85	64272.85
10-May-96	7.23	1000.00	138.31	471.27	65182.57	64182.57
10-Jun-96	7.43	1000.00	134.59	471.27	63427.99	62427.99
10-Jul-96	6.97	1000.00	143.47	471.27	67614.06	66614.06
12-Aug-96	6.65	1000.00	150.38	471.27	70867.67	69867.67
10-Sep-96	6.34	1000.00	157.73	471.27	74332.81	73332.81
10-Oct-96	5.49	1000.00	182.15	471.27	85841.53	84841.53
10-Nov-96	5.64	1000.00	177.30	471.27	83558.51	82558.51
10-Dec-96	5.15	1000.00	194.17	471.27	91508.74	90508.74
10-Jan-97	5.71	1000.00	175.13	471.27	82534.15	81534.15
10-Feb-97	5.64	1000.00	177.30	471.27	83558.51	82558.51
10-Mar-97	6.15	1000.00	162.60	471.27	76629.27	75629.27
10-Apr-97	5.91	1000.00	169.20	471.27	79741.12	78741.12
12-May-97	6.03	1000.00	165.84	471.27	78154.23	77154.23
10-Jun-97	6.03	1000.00	165.84	471.27	78154.23	77154.23
10-Jul-97	7.27	1000.00	137.55	471.27	64823.93	63823.93
11-Aug-97	7.61	1000.00	131.41	471.27	61927.73	60927.73
10-Sep-97	7.23	1000.00	138.31	471.27	65182.57	64182.57
10-Oct-97	6.89	1000.00	145.14	471.27	68399.13	67399.13
10-Nov-97	6.62	1000.00	151.06	471.27	71188.82	70188.82
10-Dec-97	6.43	1000.00	155.52	471.27	73292.38	72292.38
12-Jan-98	6.49	1000.00	154.08	471.27	72614.79	71614.79
10-Feb-98	6.28	1000.00	159.24	471.27	75042.99	74042.99
10-Mar-98	6.92	1000.00	144.51	471.27	68102.60	67102.60
10-Apr-98	8.11	1000.00	123.30	471.27	58109.74	57109.74
12-May-98	8.35	1000.00	119.76	471.27	56439.52	55439.52
10-Jun-98	7.43	1000.00	134.59	471.27	63427.99	62427.99
10-Jul-98	7.42	1000.00	134.77	471.27	63513.48	62513.48

CATEGORY: LARGE & MID-CAP ORIENTED						
Date	HDFC Equity Fund (NAV in Rs.)	Amount (Rs.)	Units	Current NAV (Rs.)	Current Value (Rs.)	Profit (Rs.)
10-Aug-98	7.43	1000.00	134.59	471.27	63427.99	62427.99
10-Sep-98	7.59	1000.00	131.75	471.27	62090.91	61090.91
12-Oct-98	7.75	1000.00	129.03	471.27	60809.03	59809.03
10-Nov-98	8.36	1000.00	119.62	471.27	56372.01	55372.01
10-Dec-98	8.73	1000.00	114.55	471.27	53982.82	52982.82
11-Jan-99	9.79	1000.00	102.15	471.27	48137.90	47137.90
10-Feb-99	10.73	1000.00	93.20	471.27	43920.78	42920.78
10-Mar-99	12.51	1000.00	79.94	471.27	37671.46	36671.46
12-Apr-99	11.94	1000.00	83.75	471.27	39469.85	38469.85
10-May-99	12.14	1000.00	82.37	471.27	38819.60	37819.60
10-Jun-99	12.69	1000.00	78.80	471.27	37137.12	36137.12
12-Jul-99	14.43	1000.00	69.30	471.27	32659.04	31659.04
10-Aug-99	16.22	1000.00	61.65	471.27	29054.87	28054.87
10-Sep-99	17.63	1000.00	56.72	471.27	26731.14	25731.14
11-Oct-99	20.14	1000.00	49.65	471.27	23399.70	22399.70
11-Nov-99	19.98	1000.00	50.05	471.27	23587.09	22587.09
10-Dec-99	21.63	1000.00	46.23	471.27	21787.79	20787.79
10-Jan-00	23.93	1000.00	41.79	471.27	19693.69	18693.69
10-Feb-00	26.80	1000.00	37.31	471.27	17584.70	16584.70
10-Mar-00	27.83	1000.00	35.93	471.27	16933.88	15933.88
10-Apr-00	24.20	1000.00	41.32	471.27	19473.97	18473.97
10-May-00	21.53	1000.00	46.45	471.27	21888.99	20888.99
12-Jun-00	21.22	1000.00	47.13	471.27	22208.77	21208.77
10-Jul-00	21.80	1000.00	45.87	471.27	21617.89	20617.89
10-Aug-00	18.86	1000.00	53.02	471.27	24987.80	23987.80
11-Sep-00	21.41	1000.00	46.71	471.27	22011.68	21011.68
10-Oct-00	18.35	1000.00	54.50	471.27	25682.29	24682.29
10-Nov-00	18.98	1000.00	52.69	471.27	24829.82	23829.82
11-Dec-00	19.44	1000.00	51.44	471.27	24242.28	23242.28
10-Jan-01	19.26	1000.00	51.92	471.27	24468.85	23468.85
12-Feb-01	20.41	1000.00	49.00	471.27	23090.15	22090.15
12-Mar-01	16.99	1000.00	58.86	471.27	27738.08	26738.08
10-Apr-01	16.60	1000.00	60.24	471.27	28389.76	27389.76
10-May-01	17.64	1000.00	56.69	471.27	26715.99	25715.99
11-Jun-01	17.65	1000.00	56.66	471.27	26700.85	25700.85
10-Jul-01	16.42	1000.00	60.90	471.27	28700.97	27700.97
10-Aug-01	16.27	1000.00	61.46	471.27	28965.58	27965.58
10-Sep-01	16.33	1000.00	61.24	471.27	28859.15	27859.15
10-Oct-01	15.10	1000.00	66.23	471.27	31209.93	30209.93
12-Nov-01	16.99	1000.00	58.86	471.27	27738.08	26738.08
10-Dec-01	19.10	1000.00	52.36	471.27	24673.82	23673.82
10-Jan-02	19.25	1000.00	51.95	471.27	24481.56	23481.56
11-Feb-02	20.68	1000.00	48.36	471.27	22788.68	21788.68

CATEGORY: LARGE & MID-CAP ORIENTED						
Date	HDFC Equity Fund (NAV in Rs.)	Amount (Rs.)	Units	Current NAV (Rs.)	Current Value (Rs.)	Profit (Rs.)
11-Mar-02	22.15	1000.00	45.15	471.27	21276.30	20276.30
10-Apr-02	22.49	1000.00	44.46	471.27	20954.65	19954.65
10-May-02	23.34	1000.00	42.84	471.27	20191.52	19191.52
10-Jun-02	22.00	1000.00	45.45	471.27	21421.36	20421.36
10-Jul-02	22.59	1000.00	44.27	471.27	20861.89	19861.89
12-Aug-02	21.34	1000.00	46.86	471.27	22083.88	21083.88
11-Sep-02	20.84	1000.00	47.98	471.27	22613.72	21613.72
10-Oct-02	20.37	1000.00	49.09	471.27	23135.49	22135.49
11-Nov-02	19.91	1000.00	50.23	471.27	23670.02	22670.02
10-Dec-02	21.67	1000.00	46.15	471.27	21747.58	20747.58
10-Jan-03	22.68	1000.00	44.09	471.27	20779.10	19779.10
10-Feb-03	22.84	1000.00	43.78	471.27	20633.54	19633.54
10-Mar-03	22.24	1000.00	44.96	471.27	21190.20	20190.20
10-Apr-03	23.49	1000.00	42.57	471.27	20062.58	19062.58
12-May-03	24.30	1000.00	41.15	471.27	19393.83	18393.83
10-Jun-03	26.64	1000.00	37.54	471.27	17690.32	16690.32
10-Jul-03	30.86	1000.00	32.41	471.27	15272.21	14272.21
11-Aug-03	33.82	1000.00	29.57	471.27	13935.07	12935.07
10-Sep-03	37.87	1000.00	26.41	471.27	12445.40	11445.40
10-Oct-03	41.81	1000.00	23.92	471.27	11271.44	10271.44
10-Nov-03	45.19	1000.00	22.13	471.27	10427.71	9427.71
10-Dec-03	47.65	1000.00	20.99	471.27	9891.07	8891.07
12-Jan-04	54.66	1000.00	18.29	471.27	8621.69	7621.69
10-Feb-04	52.75	1000.00	18.96	471.27	8934.88	7934.88
10-Mar-04	52.48	1000.00	19.06	471.27	8980.51	7980.51
12-Apr-04	54.27	1000.00	18.43	471.27	8684.28	7684.28
10-May-04	54.15	1000.00	18.47	471.27	8703.37	7703.37
10-Jun-04	47.10	1000.00	21.23	471.27	10005.52	9005.52
12-Jul-04	47.03	1000.00	21.26	471.27	10020.20	9020.20
10-Aug-04	50.70	1000.00	19.72	471.27	9295.08	8295.08
10-Sep-04	53.36	1000.00	18.74	471.27	8832.23	7832.23
11-Oct-04	56.50	1000.00	17.70	471.27	8340.62	7340.62
10-Nov-04	57.94	1000.00	17.26	471.27	8134.46	7134.46
10-Dec-04	61.26	1000.00	16.32	471.27	7693.32	6693.32
10-Jan-05	63.36	1000.00	15.78	471.27	7438.21	6438.21
10-Feb-05	66.97	1000.00	14.93	471.27	7037.45	6037.45
10-Mar-05	70.87	1000.00	14.11	471.27	6650.25	5650.25
11-Apr-05	66.65	1000.00	15.00	471.27	7070.82	6070.82
10-May-05	68.53	1000.00	14.59	471.27	6876.64	5876.64
10-Jun-05	72.46	1000.00	13.80	471.27	6503.68	5503.68
11-Jul-05	75.61	1000.00	13.23	471.27	6233.24	5233.24
10-Aug-05	83.59	1000.00	11.96	471.27	5637.94	4637.94
12-Sep-05	88.86	1000.00	11.25	471.27	5303.69	4303.69

CATEGORY: LARGE & MID-CAP ORIENTED						
Date	HDFC Equity Fund (NAV in Rs.)	Amount (Rs.)	Units	Current NAV (Rs.)	Current Value (Rs.)	Profit (Rs.)
10-Oct-05	92.95	1000.00	10.76	471.27	5070.15	4070.15
10-Nov-05	93.09	1000.00	10.74	471.27	5062.57	4062.57
12-Dec-05	104.01	1000.00	9.61	471.27	4531.01	3531.01
10-Jan-06	108.13	1000.00	9.25	471.27	4358.28	3358.28
10-Feb-06	114.19	1000.00	8.76	471.27	4127.03	3127.03
10-Mar-06	123.01	1000.00	8.13	471.27	3831.25	2831.25
10-Apr-06	130.51	1000.00	7.66	471.27	3610.96	2610.96
10-May-06	137.81	1000.00	7.26	471.27	3419.76	2419.76
12-Jun-06	104.85	1000.00	9.54	471.27	4494.71	3494.71
10-Jul-06	114.74	1000.00	8.72	471.27	4107.29	3107.29
10-Aug-06	120.30	1000.00	8.31	471.27	3917.49	2917.49
11-Sep-06	128.07	1000.00	7.81	471.27	3679.67	2679.67
10-Oct-06	134.86	1000.00	7.42	471.27	3494.62	2494.62
10-Nov-06	141.48	1000.00	7.07	471.27	3331.12	2331.12
11-Dec-06	140.67	1000.00	7.11	471.27	3350.21	2350.21
10-Jan-07	143.58	1000.00	6.96	471.27	3282.19	2282.19
12-Feb-07	150.46	1000.00	6.65	471.27	3132.17	2132.17
12-Mar-07	139.39	1000.00	7.17	471.27	3380.92	2380.92
10-Apr-07	144.48	1000.00	6.92	471.27	3261.95	2261.95
10-May-07	149.40	1000.00	6.69	471.27	3154.44	2154.44
11-Jun-07	158.85	1000.00	6.30	471.27	2966.72	1966.72
10-Jul-07	169.19	1000.00	5.91	471.27	2785.45	1785.45
10-Aug-07	166.58	1000.00	6.00	471.27	2829.06	1829.06
10-Sep-07	172.50	1000.00	5.80	471.27	2732.06	1732.06
10-Oct-07	189.83	1000.00	5.27	471.27	2482.62	1482.62
12-Nov-07	199.97	1000.00	5.00	471.27	2356.73	1356.73
10-Dec-07	213.45	1000.00	4.68	471.27	2207.86	1207.86
10-Jan-08	220.01	1000.00	4.55	471.27	2142.01	1142.01
11-Feb-08	177.14	1000.00	5.65	471.27	2660.44	1660.44
11-Mar-08	175.11	1000.00	5.71	471.27	2691.23	1691.23
10-Apr-08	166.00	1000.00	6.02	471.27	2838.96	1838.96
12-May-08	173.29	1000.00	5.77	471.27	2719.48	1719.48
10-Jun-08	158.62	1000.00	6.30	471.27	2971.16	1971.16
10-Jul-08	146.89	1000.00	6.81	471.27	3208.38	2208.38
11-Aug-08	164.53	1000.00	6.08	471.27	2864.36	1864.36
10-Sep-08	162.47	1000.00	6.16	471.27	2900.69	1900.69
10-Oct-08	117.70	1000.00	8.50	471.27	4004.06	3004.06
10-Nov-08	117.67	1000.00	8.50	471.27	4004.98	3004.98
10-Dec-08	106.56	1000.00	9.38	471.27	4422.74	3422.74
12-Jan-09	106.00	1000.00	9.43	471.27	4445.82	3445.82
10-Feb-09	106.97	1000.00	9.35	471.27	4405.59	3405.59
12-Mar-09	93.42	1000.00	10.70	471.27	5044.69	4044.69
13-Apr-09	121.22	1000.00	8.25	471.27	3887.76	2887.76

CATEGORY: LARGE & MID-CAP ORIENTED						
Date	HDFC Equity Fund (NAV in Rs.)	Amount (Rs.)	Units	Current NAV (Rs.)	Current Value (Rs.)	Profit (Rs.)
11-May-09	131.38	1000.00	7.61	471.27	3587.05	2587.05
10-Jun-09	178.02	1000.00	5.62	471.27	2647.30	1647.30
10-Jul-09	163.24	1000.00	6.13	471.27	2886.92	1886.92
10-Aug-09	179.00	1000.00	5.59	471.27	2632.79	1632.79
10-Sep-09	196.46	1000.00	5.09	471.27	2398.81	1398.81
12-Oct-09	216.44	1000.00	4.62	471.27	2177.37	1177.37
10-Nov-09	221.24	1000.00	4.52	471.27	2130.13	1130.13
10-Dec-09	228.69	1000.00	4.37	471.27	2060.74	1060.74
11-Jan-10	234.50	1000.00	4.26	471.27	2009.68	1009.68
10-Feb-10	219.46	1000.00	4.56	471.27	2147.41	1147.41
10-Mar-10	230.48	1000.00	4.34	471.27	2044.73	1044.73
12-Apr-10	239.03	1000.00	4.18	471.27	1971.59	971.59
10-May-10	238.81	1000.00	4.19	471.27	1973.41	973.41
10-Jun-10	243.89	1000.00	4.10	471.27	1932.31	932.31
12-Jul-10	257.36	1000.00	3.89	471.27	1831.17	831.17
10-Aug-10	267.80	1000.00	3.73	471.27	1759.78	759.78
13-Sep-10	287.10	1000.00	3.48	471.27	1641.49	641.49
11-Oct-10	300.19	1000.00	3.33	471.27	1569.91	569.91
10-Nov-10	312.19	1000.00	3.20	471.27	1509.56	509.56
10-Dec-10	289.22	1000.00	3.46	471.27	1629.45	629.45
10-Jan-11	282.22	1000.00	3.54	471.27	1669.87	669.87
10-Feb-11	256.55	1000.00	3.90	471.27	1836.95	836.95
10-Mar-11	267.14	1000.00	3.74	471.27	1764.13	764.13
11-Apr-11	284.25	1000.00	3.52	471.27	1657.97	657.97
10-May-11	278.81	1000.00	3.59	471.27	1690.32	690.32
10-Jun-11	277.24	1000.00	3.61	471.27	1699.84	699.84
11-Jul-11	281.27	1000.00	3.56	471.27	1675.54	675.54
10-Aug-11	262.56	1000.00	3.81	471.27	1794.92	794.92
12-Sep-11	245.47	1000.00	4.07	471.27	1919.88	919.88
10-Oct-11	244.04	1000.00	4.10	471.27	1931.12	931.12
11.11.11	246.75	1000.00	4.05	471.27	1909.91	909.91
12.12.11	228.95	1000.00	4.37	471.27	2058.40	1058.40
10.01.12	229.09	1000.00	4.37	471.27	2057.14	1057.14
10.02.12	260.84	1000.00	3.83	471.27	1806.74	806.74
12.03.12	264.00	1000.00	3.79	471.27	1785.11	785.11
10.04.12	259.16	1000.00	3.86	471.27	1818.45	818.45
10.05.12	242.47	1000.00	4.12	471.27	1943.62	943.62
11.06.12	247.97	1000.00	4.03	471.27	1900.51	900.51
10.07.12	262.17	1000.00	3.81	471.27	1797.57	797.57
10.08.12	253.28	1000.00	3.95	471.27	1860.67	860.67
10.09.12	255.33	1000.00	3.92	471.27	1845.73	845.73
10.10.12	276.83	1000.00	3.61	471.27	1702.38	702.38
09.11.12	275.78	1000.00	3.63	471.27	1708.86	708.86

CATEGORY: LARGE & MID-CAP ORIENTED						
Date	HDFC Equity Fund (NAV in Rs.)	Amount (Rs.)	Units	Current NAV (Rs.)	Current Value (Rs.)	Profit (Rs.)
10.12.12	291.43	1000.00	3.43	471.27	1617.10	617.10
10.01.13	299.26	1000.00	3.34	471.27	1574.78	574.78
11.02.13	288.71	1000.00	3.46	471.27	1632.33	632.33
11.03.13	286.04	1000.00	3.50	471.27	1647.57	647.57
11.04.13	269.76	1000.00	3.71	471.27	1747.00	747.00
10-May-13	289.02	1000.00	3.46	471.27	1630.58	630.58
10-Jun-13	278.47	1000.00	3.59	471.27	1692.35	692.35
10-Jul-13	266.16	1000.00	3.76	471.27	1770.63	770.63
12-Aug-13	248.31	1000.00	4.03	471.27	1897.91	897.91
10-Sep-13	260.72	1000.00	3.84	471.27	1807.57	807.57
10-Oct-13	269.15	1000.00	3.72	471.27	1750.96	750.96
10-Nov-13	282.70	1000.00	3.54	471.27	1667.03	667.03
10-Dec-13	299.96	1000.00	3.33	471.27	1571.11	571.11
10-Jan-14	295.82	1000.00	3.38	471.27	1593.10	593.10
10-Feb-14	289.92	1000.00	3.45	471.27	1625.52	625.52
10-Mar-14	318.89	1000.00	3.14	471.27	1477.85	477.85
10-Apr-14	342.44	1000.00	2.92	471.27	1376.21	376.21
9-May-14	353.48	1000.00	2.83	471.27	1333.23	333.23
10-Jun-14	422.22	1000.00	2.37	471.27	1116.17	116.17
10-Jul-14	416.56	1000.00	2.40	471.27	1131.34	131.34
11-Aug-14	418.12	1000.00	2.39	471.27	1127.12	127.12
10-Sep-14	454.45	1000.00	2.20	471.27	1037.01	37.01
10-Oct-14	439.62	1000.00	2.27	471.27	1071.99	71.99
10-Nov-14	468.81	1000.00	2.13	471.27	1005.25	5.25
10-Dec-14	471.27	1000.00	2.12	471.27	1000.00	0.00
	TOTAL	240000.00	10726.78		5055210.12	4815210.12

CATEGORY: BALANCED FUND (Equity Hybrid; about 65% in equity stocks & 35% in debt)						
Date	HDFC Prudence Fund (NAV in Rs.)	Amount (Rs.)	Units	Current NAV (Rs.)	Current Value (Rs.)	Profit (Rs.)
25-Feb-94	9.98	1000.00	100.20	369.43	37017.03	36017.03
24-Mar-94	10.12	1000.00	98.81	369.43	36504.94	35504.94
22-Apr-94	10.15	1000.00	98.52	369.43	36397.04	35397.04
20-May-94	10.49	1000.00	95.33	369.43	35217.35	34217.35
20-Jun-94	10.57	1000.00	94.61	369.43	34950.80	33950.80
20-Jul-94	10.48	1000.00	95.42	369.43	35250.95	34250.95
24-Aug-94	10.98	1000.00	91.07	369.43	33645.72	32645.72
20-Sep-94	11.47	1000.00	87.18	369.43	32208.37	31208.37
20-Oct-94	12.23	1000.00	81.77	369.43	30206.87	29206.87
21-Nov-94	12.58	1000.00	79.49	369.43	29366.45	28366.45
20-Dec-94	12.89	1000.00	77.58	369.43	28660.20	27660.20
20-Jan-95	11.01	1000.00	90.83	369.43	33554.04	32554.04
20-Feb-95	10.10	1000.00	99.01	369.43	36577.23	35577.23
23-Mar-95	10.44	1000.00	95.79	369.43	35386.02	34386.02
21-Apr-95	10.19	1000.00	98.14	369.43	36254.17	35254.17
22-May-95	9.54	1000.00	104.82	369.43	38724.32	37724.32
20-Jun-95	9.50	1000.00	105.26	369.43	38887.37	37887.37
20-Jul-95	9.41	1000.00	106.27	369.43	39259.30	38259.30
21-Aug-95	9.12	1000.00	109.65	369.43	40507.68	39507.68
20-Sep-95	8.97	1000.00	111.48	369.43	41185.06	40185.06
23-Oct-95	8.91	1000.00	112.23	369.43	41462.40	40462.40
20-Nov-95	8.51	1000.00	117.51	369.43	43411.28	42411.28
22-Dec-95	8.55	1000.00	116.96	369.43	43208.19	42208.19
20-Jan-96	8.21	1000.00	121.80	369.43	44997.56	43997.56
20-Feb-96	8.65	1000.00	115.61	369.43	42708.67	41708.67
21-Mar-96	8.27	1000.00	120.92	369.43	44671.10	43671.10
22-Apr-96	8.75	1000.00	114.29	369.43	42220.57	41220.57
20-May-96	8.67	1000.00	115.34	369.43	42610.15	41610.15
20-Jun-96	8.95	1000.00	111.73	369.43	41277.09	40277.09
22-Jul-96	8.78	1000.00	113.90	369.43	42076.31	41076.31
20-Aug-96	8.30	1000.00	120.48	369.43	44509.64	43509.64
20-Sep-96	8.14	1000.00	122.85	369.43	45384.52	44384.52
22-Oct-96	8.79	1000.00	113.77	369.43	42028.44	41028.44
20-Nov-96	8.69	1000.00	115.07	369.43	42512.08	41512.08
20-Dec-96	8.69	1000.00	115.07	369.43	42512.08	41512.08
20-Jan-97	9.13	1000.00	109.53	369.43	40463.31	39463.31
20-Feb-97	9.14	1000.00	109.41	369.43	40419.04	39419.04
20-Mar-97	9.28	1000.00	107.76	369.43	39809.27	38809.27
21-Apr-97	9.40	1000.00	106.38	369.43	39301.06	38301.06
20-May-97	9.37	1000.00	106.72	369.43	39426.89	38426.89
21-Jun-97	9.56	1000.00	104.60	369.43	38643.31	37643.31
20-Jul-97	10.06	1000.00	99.40	369.43	36722.66	35722.66
20-Aug-97	10.33	1000.00	96.81	369.43	35762.83	34762.83

CATEGORY: BALANCED FUND (Equity Hybrid; about 65% in equity stocks & 35% in debt)						
Date	HDFC Prudence Fund (NAV in Rs.)	Amount (Rs.)	Units	Current NAV (Rs.)	Current Value (Rs.)	Profit (Rs.)
22-Sep-97	10.07	1000.00	99.30	369.43	36686.20	35686.20
20-Oct-97	10.47	1000.00	95.51	369.43	35284.62	34284.62
20-Nov-97	10.09	1000.00	99.11	369.43	36613.48	35613.48
22-Dec-97	10.34	1000.00	96.71	369.43	35728.24	34728.24
20-Jan-98	10.47	1000.00	95.51	369.43	35284.62	34284.62
20-Feb-98	10.32	1000.00	96.90	369.43	35797.48	34797.48
20-Mar-98	10.98	1000.00	91.07	369.43	33645.72	32645.72
20-Apr-98	12.19	1000.00	82.03	369.43	30305.99	29305.99
20-May-98	12.18	1000.00	82.10	369.43	30330.87	29330.87
22-Jun-98	10.89	1000.00	91.83	369.43	33923.78	32923.78
20-Jul-98	11.46	1000.00	87.26	369.43	32236.47	31236.47
20-Aug-98	11.41	1000.00	87.64	369.43	32377.74	31377.74
21-Sep-98	11.60	1000.00	86.21	369.43	31847.41	30847.41
20-Oct-98	10.33	1000.00	96.81	369.43	35762.83	34762.83
20-Jan-98	10.47	1000.00	95.51	369.43	35284.62	34284.62
20-Nov-98	10.56	1000.00	94.70	369.43	34983.90	33983.90
20-Dec-98	10.96	1000.00	91.24	369.43	33707.12	32707.12
20-Jan-99	11.06	1000.00	90.42	369.43	33402.35	32402.35
22-Feb-99	10.91	1000.00	91.66	369.43	33861.59	32861.59
22-Mar-99	12.61	1000.00	79.30	369.43	29296.59	28296.59
31-Mar-99	13.02	1000.00	76.80	369.43	28374.04	27374.04
20-May-99	14.44	1000.00	69.25	369.43	25583.80	24583.80
21-Jun-99	14.30	1000.00	69.93	369.43	25834.27	24834.27
20-Jul-99	16.20	1000.00	61.73	369.43	22804.32	21804.32
20-Aug-99	17.85	1000.00	56.02	369.43	20696.36	19696.36
20-Sep-99	18.19	1000.00	54.98	369.43	20309.51	19309.51
20-Oct-99	20.66	1000.00	48.40	369.43	17881.41	16881.41
22-Nov-99	20.16	1000.00	49.60	369.43	18324.90	17324.90
20-Dec-99	21.31	1000.00	46.93	369.43	17335.99	16335.99
20-Jan-00	23.10	1000.00	43.29	369.43	15992.64	14992.64
21-Feb-00	22.58	1000.00	44.29	369.43	16360.94	15360.94
20-Mar-00	20.28	1000.00	49.31	369.43	18216.47	17216.47
20-Apr-00	19.65	1000.00	50.89	369.43	18800.51	17800.51
22-May-00	18.50	1000.00	54.05	369.43	19969.19	18969.19
20-Jun-00	20.80	1000.00	48.08	369.43	17761.06	16761.06
20-Jul-00	19.53	1000.00	51.20	369.43	18916.03	17916.03
21-Aug-00	19.56	1000.00	51.12	369.43	18887.01	17887.01
20-Sep-00	19.16	1000.00	52.19	369.43	19281.32	18281.32
20-Oct-00	18.61	1000.00	53.73	369.43	19851.16	18851.16
20-Nov-00	19.52	1000.00	51.23	369.43	18925.72	17925.72
20-Dec-00	20.01	1000.00	49.98	369.43	18462.27	17462.27
22-Jan-01	20.17	1000.00	49.58	369.43	18315.82	17315.82
20-Feb-01	20.71	1000.00	48.29	369.43	17838.24	16838.24

CATEGORY: BALANCED FUND (Equity Hybrid; about 65% in equity stocks & 35% in debt)						
Date	HDFC Prudence Fund (NAV in Rs.)	Amount (Rs.)	Units	Current NAV (Rs.)	Current Value (Rs.)	Profit (Rs.)
20-Mar-01	17.74	1000.00	56.37	369.43	20824.69	19824.69
20-Apr-01	17.44	1000.00	57.34	369.43	21182.91	20182.91
21-May-01	18.08	1000.00	55.31	369.43	20433.08	19433.08
20-Jun-01	17.81	1000.00	56.15	369.43	20742.84	19742.84
20-Jul-01	17.20	1000.00	58.14	369.43	21478.49	20478.49
20-Aug-01	17.53	1000.00	57.05	369.43	21074.16	20074.16
20-Sep-01	16.35	1000.00	61.16	369.43	22595.11	21595.11
22-Oct-01	17.34	1000.00	57.67	369.43	21305.07	20305.07
20-Nov-01	18.82	1000.00	53.13	369.43	19629.65	18629.65
20-Dec-01	19.15	1000.00	52.22	369.43	19291.38	18291.38
20-Jan-02	20.33	1000.00	49.19	369.43	18171.67	17171.67
20-Feb-02	21.46	1000.00	46.60	369.43	17214.82	16214.82
20-Mar-02	22.06	1000.00	45.33	369.43	16746.60	15746.60
22-Apr-02	22.34	1000.00	44.76	369.43	16536.71	15536.71
20-May-02	22.21	1000.00	45.02	369.43	16633.50	15633.50
20-Jun-02	22.44	1000.00	44.56	369.43	16463.01	15463.01
22-Jul-02	22.44	1000.00	44.56	369.43	16463.01	15463.01
20-Aug-02	22.48	1000.00	44.48	369.43	16433.72	15433.72
20-Sep-02	21.24	1000.00	47.08	369.43	17393.13	16393.13
21-Oct-02	21.55	1000.00	46.40	369.43	17142.92	16142.92
20-Nov-02	22.10	1000.00	45.25	369.43	16716.29	15716.29
20-Dec-02	23.43	1000.00	42.68	369.43	15767.39	14767.39
20-Jan-03	24.59	1000.00	40.67	369.43	15023.59	14023.59
20-Feb-03	24.88	1000.00	40.19	369.43	14848.47	13848.47
20-Mar-03	24.34	1000.00	41.08	369.43	15177.90	14177.90
21-Apr-03	25.60	1000.00	39.06	369.43	14430.86	13430.86
20-May-03	27.55	1000.00	36.30	369.43	13409.44	12409.44
20-Jun-03	30.34	1000.00	32.96	369.43	12176.33	11176.33
20-Jul-03	31.92	1000.00	31.33	369.43	11573.62	10573.62
20-Aug-03	34.99	1000.00	28.58	369.43	10558.16	9558.16
22-Sep-03	34.99	1000.00	28.58	369.43	10558.16	9558.16
20-Oct-03	39.22	1000.00	25.50	369.43	9419.43	8419.43
20-Nov-03	40.64	1000.00	24.61	369.43	9090.31	8090.31
20-Dec-03	44.95	1000.00	22.25	369.43	8218.69	7218.69
20-Jan-04	46.96	1000.00	21.29	369.43	7866.91	6866.91
20-Feb-04	46.13	1000.00	21.68	369.43	8008.45	7008.45
20-Mar-04	43.38	1000.00	23.05	369.43	8516.14	7516.14
20-Apr-04	47.58	1000.00	21.02	369.43	7764.40	6764.40
20-May-04	44.50	1000.00	22.47	369.43	8301.80	7301.80
21-Jun-04	42.00	1000.00	23.81	369.43	8795.95	7795.95
20-Jul-04	44.56	1000.00	22.44	369.43	8290.62	7290.62
20-Aug-04	45.49	1000.00	21.98	369.43	8121.13	7121.13
20-Sep-04	49.24	1000.00	20.31	369.43	7502.64	6502.64

CATEGORY: BALANCED FUND (Equity Hybrid; about 65% in equity stocks & 35% in debt)						
Date	HDFC Prudence Fund (NAV in Rs.)	Amount (Rs.)	Units	Current NAV (Rs.)	Current Value (Rs.)	Profit (Rs.)
20-Oct-04	49.60	1000.00	20.16	369.43	7448.19	6448.19
20-Nov-04	52.24	1000.00	19.14	369.43	7071.78	6071.78
20-Dec-04	59.95	1000.00	16.68	369.43	6162.30	5162.30
20-Jan-05	55.02	1000.00	18.18	369.43	6714.47	5714.47
21-Feb-05	59.07	1000.00	16.93	369.43	6254.11	5254.11
21-Mar-05	60.45	1000.00	16.54	369.43	6111.33	5111.33
20-Apr-05	59.50	1000.00	16.81	369.43	6208.91	5208.91
20-May-05	63.65	1000.00	15.71	369.43	5804.08	4804.08
20-Jun-05	64.12	1000.00	15.60	369.43	5761.54	4761.54
20-Jul-05	68.39	1000.00	14.62	369.43	5401.81	4401.81
22-Aug-05	72.71	1000.00	13.75	369.43	5080.87	4080.87
20-Sep-05	78.19	1000.00	12.79	369.43	4724.77	3724.77
20-Oct-05	74.67	1000.00	13.39	369.43	4947.50	3947.50
21-Nov-05	79.57	1000.00	12.57	369.43	4642.83	3642.83
20-Dec-05	84.27	1000.00	11.87	369.43	4383.89	3383.89
20-Jan-06	86.73	1000.00	11.53	369.43	4259.54	3259.54
20-Feb-06	88.18	1000.00	11.34	369.43	4189.50	3189.50
20-Mar-06	94.19	1000.00	10.62	369.43	3922.18	2922.18
20-Apr-06	96.70	1000.00	10.34	369.43	3820.37	2820.37
22-May-06	90.45	1000.00	11.06	369.43	4084.36	3084.36
20-Jun-06	85.70	1000.00	11.67	369.43	4310.74	3310.74
20-Jul-06	87.18	1000.00	11.47	369.43	4237.55	3237.55
21-Aug-06	96.37	1000.00	10.38	369.43	3833.45	2833.45
20-Sep-06	100.77	1000.00	9.92	369.43	3666.07	2666.07
20-Oct-06	105.36	1000.00	9.49	369.43	3506.36	2506.36
20-Nov-06	107.76	1000.00	9.28	369.43	3428.27	2428.27
20-Dec-06	110.63	1000.00	9.04	369.43	3339.33	2339.33
22-Jan-07	116.94	1000.00	8.55	369.43	3159.14	2159.14
20-Feb-07	115.52	1000.00	8.66	369.43	3197.97	2197.97
20-Mar-07	108.06	1000.00	9.25	369.43	3418.75	2418.75
20-Apr-07	114.25	1000.00	8.75	369.43	3233.52	2233.52
20-May-07	118.78	1000.00	8.42	369.43	3110.20	2110.20
20-Jun-07	123.00	1000.00	8.13	369.43	3003.50	2003.50
23-Jul-07	130.36	1000.00	7.67	369.43	2833.92	1833.92
20-Aug-07	125.32	1000.00	7.98	369.43	2947.89	1947.89
20-Sep-07	132.95	1000.00	7.52	369.43	2778.71	1778.71
22-Oct-07	135.06	1000.00	7.40	369.43	2735.30	1735.30
20-Nov-07	153.66	1000.00	6.51	369.43	2404.20	1404.20
20-Dec-07	155.55	1000.00	6.43	369.43	2374.99	1374.99
21-Jan-08	147.61	1000.00	6.77	369.43	2502.74	1502.74
20-Feb-08	141.06	1000.00	7.09	369.43	2618.96	1618.96
24-Mar-08	121.74	1000.00	8.21	369.43	3034.58	2034.58
20-Apr-08	127.70	1000.00	7.83	369.43	2892.95	1892.95

CATEGORY: BALANCED FUND (Equity Hybrid; about 65% in equity stocks & 35% in debt)						
Date	HDFC Prudence Fund (NAV in Rs.)	Amount (Rs.)	Units	Current NAV (Rs.)	Current Value (Rs.)	Profit (Rs.)
20-May-08	132.03	1000.00	7.57	369.43	2798.08	1798.08
20-Jun-08	120.21	1000.00	8.32	369.43	3073.21	2073.21
21-Jul-08	112.91	1000.00	8.86	369.43	3271.90	2271.90
20-Aug-08	120.49	1000.00	8.30	369.43	3066.06	2066.06
22-Sep-08	119.10	1000.00	8.40	369.43	3101.85	2101.85
20-Oct-08	96.10	1000.00	10.41	369.43	3844.22	2844.22
20-Nov-08	84.61	1000.00	11.82	369.43	4366.27	3366.27
22-Dec-08	94.57	1000.00	10.57	369.43	3906.42	2906.42
20-Jan-09	89.75	1000.00	11.14	369.43	4116.21	3116.21
20-Feb-09	84.99	1000.00	11.77	369.43	4346.75	3346.75
20-Mar-09	86.17	1000.00	11.60	369.43	4287.22	3287.22
20-Apr-09	103.48	1000.00	9.66	369.43	3570.06	2570.06
20-May-09	126.71	1000.00	7.89	369.43	2915.56	1915.56
22-Jun-09	132.11	1000.00	7.57	369.43	2796.38	1796.38
20-Jul-09	140.04	1000.00	7.14	369.43	2638.03	1638.03
21-Aug-09	144.61	1000.00	6.92	369.43	2554.66	1554.66
20-Sep-09	158.67	1000.00	6.30	369.43	2328.29	1328.29
20-Oct-09	165.34	1000.00	6.05	369.43	2234.37	1234.37
20-Nov-09	169.74	1000.00	5.89	369.43	2176.45	1176.45
20-Dec-09	169.74	1000.00	5.89	369.43	2176.45	1176.45
20-Jan-10	177.84	1000.00	5.62	369.43	2077.32	1077.32
22-Feb-10	172.05	1000.00	5.81	369.43	2147.22	1147.22
22-Mar-10	179.96	1000.00	5.56	369.43	2052.85	1052.85
22-Apr-10	185.168	1000.00	5.40	369.43	1995.11	995.11
20-May-10	186.70	1000.00	5.36	369.43	1978.74	978.74
20-Jun-10	193.70	1000.00	5.16	369.43	1907.23	907.23
20-Jul-10	200.60	1000.00	4.99	369.43	1841.63	841.63
20-Aug-10	207.05	1000.00	4.83	369.43	1784.30	784.30
20-Sep-10	216.31	1000.00	4.62	369.43	1707.87	707.87
20-Oct-10	217.32	1000.00	4.60	369.43	1699.94	699.94
22-Nov-10	221.91	1000.00	4.51	369.43	1664.81	664.81
20-Dec-10	215.68	1000.00	4.64	369.43	1712.88	712.88
20-Jan-11	210.04	1000.00	4.76	369.43	1758.83	758.83
21-Feb-11	205.93	1000.00	4.86	369.43	1793.92	793.92
21-Mar-11	202.20	1000.00	4.95	369.43	1827.05	827.05
20-Apr-11	217.49	1000.00	4.60	369.43	1698.61	698.61
20-May-11	210.16	1000.00	4.76	369.43	1757.85	757.85
20-Jun-11	209.99	1000.00	4.76	369.43	1759.27	759.27
20-Jul-11	218.50	1000.00	4.58	369.43	1690.76	690.76
22-Aug-11	203.50	1000.00	4.91	369.43	1815.38	815.38
20-Sep-11	207.68	1000.00	4.82	369.43	1778.84	778.84
20-Oct-11	203.64	1000.00	4.91	369.43	1814.13	814.13
21-Nov-11	191.81	1000.00	5.21	369.43	1926.02	926.02

CATEGORY: BALANCED FUND (Equity Hybrid; about 65% in equity stocks & 35% in debt)						
Date	HDFC Prudence Fund (NAV in Rs.)	Amount (Rs.)	Units	Current NAV (Rs.)	Current Value (Rs.)	Profit (Rs.)
20-Dec-11	183.13	1000.00	5.46	369.43	2017.31	1017.31
20-Jan-12	199.93	1000.00	5.00	369.43	1847.80	847.80
21-Feb-12	220.17	1000.00	4.54	369.43	1677.93	677.93
20-Mar-12	213.06	1000.00	4.69	369.43	1733.92	733.92
20-Apr-12	217.97	1000.00	4.59	369.43	1694.87	694.87
21-May-12	205.18	1000.00	4.87	369.43	1800.52	800.52
20-Jun-12	209.33	1000.00	4.78	369.43	1764.82	764.82
20-Jul-12	214.68	1000.00	4.66	369.43	1720.84	720.84
21-Aug-12	214.19	1000.00	4.67	369.43	1724.78	724.78
20-Sep-12	221.11	1000.00	4.52	369.43	1670.80	670.80
22-Oct-12	230.50	1000.00	4.34	369.43	1602.73	602.73
20-Nov-12	223.68	1000.00	4.47	369.43	1651.60	651.60
20-Dec-12	238.66	1000.00	4.19	369.43	1547.93	547.93
21-Jan-13	245.88	1000.00	4.07	369.43	1502.48	502.48
20-Feb-13	233.67	1000.00	4.28	369.43	1580.99	580.99
20-Mar-13	222.85	1000.00	4.49	369.43	1657.75	657.75
22-Apr-13	228.54	1000.00	4.38	369.43	1616.48	616.48
20-May-13	239.18	1000.00	4.18	369.43	1544.57	544.57
20-Jun-13	223.74	1000.00	4.47	369.43	1651.16	651.16
19-Jul-13	219.20	1000.00	4.56	369.43	1685.36	685.36
20-Aug-13	198.98	1000.00	5.03	369.43	1856.62	856.62
20-Sep-13	214.96	1000.00	4.65	369.43	1718.60	718.60
21-Oct-13	224.04	1000.00	4.46	369.43	1648.95	648.95
20-Nov-13	232.73	1000.00	4.30	369.43	1587.38	587.38
20-Dec-13	242.89	1000.00	4.12	369.43	1520.98	520.98
20-Jan-14	244.57	1000.00	4.09	369.43	1510.53	510.53
20-Feb-14	239.83	1000.00	4.17	369.43	1540.38	540.38
20-Mar-14	254.13	1000.00	3.93	369.43	1453.70	453.70
21-Apr-14	276.43	1000.00	3.62	369.43	1336.43	336.43
20-May-14	308.36	1000.00	3.24	369.43	1198.05	198.05
20-Jun-14	330.20	1000.00	3.03	369.43	1118.81	118.81
21-Jul-14	338.41	1000.00	2.95	369.43	1091.66	91.66
20-Aug-14	343.93	1000.00	2.91	369.43	1074.14	74.14
19-Sep-14	360.31	1000.00	2.78	369.43	1025.31	25.31
20-Oct-14	350.59	1000.00	2.85	369.43	1053.74	53.74
20-Nov-14	375.42	1000.00	2.66	369.43	984.04	-15.96
19-Dec-14	369.43	1000.00	2.71	369.43	1000.00	0.00
	TOTAL	252000.00	10195.74		3766613.48	3514613.48

MODEL SYSTEMATIC INVESTMENT PLAN (SIP) PORTFOLIO DESIGN ACROSS TYPES OF INVESTORS							
Monthly Total Investment (Rs.)	**5000**						
Themes & Exposure - 1 (Conservative)	**Exposure %**		**Themes & Exposure - 2 (Moderatively Aggressively)**	**Exposure %**		**Themes & Exposure - 3 (Aggressive)**	**Exposure %**
Balanced Fund	**10%**		Balanced Fund	**10%**		Balanced Fund	**0%**
Index Fund	**15%**		Index Fund	**0%**		Index Fund	**0%**
Large-cap oriented fund	**35%**		Large-cap oriented	**25%**		Large-cap oriented fund	**10%**
Multi-cap Fund (regular)	**30%**		Multi-cap (regular/opprtunstc)	**25%**		Multi-cap (regular/opprtunstc)	**20%**
Mid-cap oriented fund	**0%**		Mid-cap oriented	**20%**		Mid/Small cap oriented funds	**40%**
Large & Mid-cap oriented fund	**10%**		Large & Mid-cap oriented	**20%**		Large & Mid-cap oriented fund	**20%**
Mid & Small Cap oriented	**0%**		Mid & Small Cap oriented	**0%**		Thematic / Sector-based Funds	**10%**
	100%			**100%**			**100%**
Expected returns range (CAGR)	**12% - 15%**		**Expected returns range (CAGR)**	**15% - 18%**		**Expected returns range (CAGR)**	**18% plus**

Indicative Schemes								
Schemes	**Amount**	**Dates**	Schemes	**Amount**	**Dates**	Schemes	**Amount**	**Dates**
ICICI Pru Balanced Fund	**500.00**	1st	HDFC Prudence Fund	**500.00**	1st	NA	**0.00**	
Franklin India Nifty Plan	**750.00**	5th	NA	**0.00**		NA	**0.00**	
Birla SL Top 100 Fund	**1750.00**	10th	Birla SL Frontline Equity Fund	**1250.00**	5th	UTI Opportunities Fund	**500.00**	1st
DSP BR Equity Fund	**1500.00**	15th	Reliance Equity Opportunities Fund	**1250.00**	10th	Kotak Opportunities Fund	**1000.00**	5th
NA	**0.00**		Franklin India Prima Plus	**1000.00**	15th	DSP BR Micro Cap Fund	**2000.00**	10th
HDFC Equity Fund	**500.00**	20th	Kotak Select Focus Fund	**1000.00**	20th	Mirae India Asset Oppr. Fund	**1000.00**	15th
NA	**0.00**		NA	**0.00**		Reliance Banking Fund	**500.00**	20th
Total	**5000.00**		**Total**	**5000.00**		**Total**	**5000.00**	

THEME DIFFERENTIATOR DATA TO PROVE THAT EACH THEME IS DESIGNED TO MEET SPECIFIC RISK PROFILE OF INVESTORS					
		NAV DATES (ONE YEAR)			
FUND & SCHEME NAME	THEME TYPE	NAV ON 01.01.2014	NAV ON 31.12.2014	Returns in % (absolute)	Indicative Style of Management
DSP BR EQUITY FUND	Large Cap Oriented	113.58	156.2	**37.52**	Conservative
DSP BR OPPORTUNITIES FUND	Multi Cap - Opportunistic	96.61	140.22	**45.14**	Moderately Aggressive
DSP BR MID & SMALL CAP FUND	Mid & Small Cap Oriented	20.60	34.97	**69.76**	Aggressive
FRANKLIN INDIA BLUECHIP FUND	Large Cap Oriented	246.76	338.00	**36.98**	Conservative
FRANKLIN INDIA PRIMA PLUS FUND	Large & Mid Cap Oriented	266.75	417.60	**56.55**	Moderately Aggressive
FRANKLIN INDIA PRIMA FUND	Mid & Small Cap Oriented	355.95	632.40	**77.67**	Aggressive
HDFC TOP 200 FUND	Large Cap Oriented	235.41	344.90	**46.51**	Conservative
HDFC MID CAP OPPR. FUND	Mid Cap Oriented	20.51	36.09	**75.96**	Aggressive
ICICI PRU FOCUSSED BLUECHIP FUND	Large Cap Oriented	20.32	28.63	**40.90**	Conservative
ICICI PRU VALUE DISCOVERY FUND	Mid Cap Oriented	62.58	107.99	**72.56**	Aggressive
KOTAK 50 FUND	Large Cap Oriented	115.03	163.78	**42.38**	Conservative
KOTAK EQUITY OPPORTUNITIES FUND	Multi Cap - Opportunistic	52.35	78.45	**49.86**	Moderately Aggressive
KOTAK MID-CAP FUND	Mid Cap Oriented	28.78	49.93	**73.49**	Aggressive
RELIANCE RSF EQUITY FUND	Multi Cap - Regular	32.93	51.08	**55.12**	Conservative
RELIANCE EQUITY OPPR. FUND	Multi Cap - Opportunistic	46.35	74.03	**59.72**	Moderately Aggressive
UTI EQUITY FUND	Large Cap Oriented	67.42	99.00	**46.84**	Conservative
UTI MID CAP FUND	Mid & Small Cap Oriented	39.79	75.43	**89.57**	Aggressive
UTI BANKING FUND	Sector Fund - Banking	42.07	69	**64.01**	Ultra Aggressive
RELIANCE PHARMA FUND	Sector Fund - Pharma	84.60	125.61	**48.48**	Ultra Aggressive
DSP BR T.I.G.E.R FUND	Thematic - Infrastructure	42.17	67.65	**60.42**	Ultra Aggressive
FRANKLIN BUILD INDIA FUND	Thematic - Infrastructure	14.48	27.87	**92.47**	Ultra Aggressive
Note: The above compilation is to explain the fact that each of the themes designed by a fund house is to offer objective based returns to investors. Since Large Cap is generally considered to be low on risk compared to Mid Cap, such differences can be understood from the returns each of these themes have generated which further proves a fact that lower the risk lower the return and higher the risk higher the return. The data also helps the investors to invest as a portfolio by picking different types of themes to meet their returns expectations.					

EDUCATION INFLATION AT 7.50% ANNUAL INCREASE OF FEE (INDICATIVE)			
Child's future education flow	Current Cost (Rs.)	Future Cost (with inflation; in Rs.)	Purpose
Stage 1: Pre Nursery			
Current Tuition Fee (year 2015)	50000 / year		
2018		62000	Lower Kindergarten
2019		67000	Upper Kindergarten
Stage 2: Primary Schooling			
Current Tuition Fee (year 2015)	100000 / year		
2020		144000	1st Standard
2021		155000	2nd Standard
2022		166000	3rd Standard
2023		178000	4th Standard
Stage 3: Middle Schooling	100000 / year		
2024		191000	5th standard
2025		205000	6th Standard
2026		220000	7th Standard
Stage 4: High Schooling	100000 / year		
2027		236000	8th Standard
2028		254000	9th Standard
2029		273000	10th Standard
Stage 5: Pre University (PU)			
Current Tuition Fee (year 2015)	35000 / year		
2030		104000	1st PU
2031		112000	2nd PU
Stage 6: Under Graduation (Commerce)			
Current Tuition Fee (year 2015)	80000 / year		
2032		273000	1st Year
2033		293000	2nd Year
2034		315000	3rd Year
Stage 7: Post Graduation (MBA)			
Current Tuition Fee (year 2015)	700000 / 2 yrs		
2035-37		3000000	2 year MBA
TOTAL		**6248000**	
Note: The above data is compiled on the assumption that the child is born in 2015 and its first stage of education starts when the child is 3 year old. The inflation is based on the cost of tuition fee as charged by a private/convent school / college in Bangalore Urban area. The raise in the fee fee year-on-year may change or vary from institution to institution.			

A brief profile about the author

Balaji Rao D G, 49 years, is a Professor and Associate Dean at Jain College, Bangalore. He has studied B.Com, MBA, PGDMM, PGDFA and a Research Scholar pursuing his PhD from Jain University. He has a versatile back-ground with 23 years of industry experience and 5 years of academic exposure and has been associated with financial markets and investments related field for over 18 years and has experience of handling and managing investments of small, medium & large investors during his tenure including institutional investors. He has worked in senior positions at renowned brands like Karvy (7 years), Escorts (3 years), CCSIL-Citigroup (1 year), Apple Credit Corpn. (4 years), Gayathri & Co - Stock Brokers (3 years) and A.A. Property Developers (5 years). His last assignment was at Karvy Stock Broking Ltd. as an AVP & Zonal Head - Distribution (Jan 2010).

He has authored four editions of book "Financial Markets & Investment Instruments" (a textbook for MBA students) that has sold over 3000 copies.

Further, he has conducted various Investor Awareness Programs at many locations in Bangalore and at other up-country locations and also has hosted various TV live phone-in programs and Radio programs in his endeavour to reach out to create awareness on investment products, besides appearing as a market expert on national TV channels on invitation.

His photo/articles have appeared in Business Line & Mid-Day newspapers. He has been a visiting professor at Jain College, Jain University, Christ University, XIME, Garden City College of Management and such other reputed B-Schools.

He specializes in teaching Financial Markets & Instruments / Financial Planning & Wealth Management subjects. He has shared his thoughts on investments for organizations like CII, Rotary Clubs, Management Associations and other forums. He has conducted corporate training sessions on Financial Planning & Investment Management for clients of NJ India Invest, UTI Mutual Fund, Franklin Templeton Mutual Fund, Lotus Knowlwealth and Stock Market Institute among other premier institutes in the past.

He also regularly writes "CASHWISE" column for the national daily "The Hindu" newspaper's supplement "Property Plus" that appears every Saturday.

www.ingramcontent.com/pod-product-compliance
Lightning Source LLC
Chambersburg PA
CBHW032009170526
45157CB00002B/609

* 9 7 8 1 4 8 2 8 4 7 8 2 6 *